PAUL THOMAS YOUNG is Professor of Psychology Emeritus at the University of Illinois at Urbana. He is the author of four other books dealing with the dynamics of feeling and emotion: *Motivation of Behavior, Emotion in Man and Animal, Motivation and Emotion,* and *Emotion in Man and Animal: Its Nature and Dynamic Basis.* He has published numerous experimental and theoretical papers in psychological journals, a dozen encyclopedia articles, and chapters on motivation in several textbooks.

Understanding Your Feelings and Emotions

PAUL THOMAS YOUNG

Professor Emeritus of Psychology
University of Illinois at Urbana

A SPECTRUM BOOK

PRENTICE-HALL, INC., ENGLEWOOD CLIFFS, NEW JERSEY

Library of Congress Cataloging in Publication Data

Young, Paul Thomas, 1892–
  Understanding your feelings and emotions.

  (A Spectrum book)
  Bibliography: p.
  Includes index.
  1. Emotions.   I.   Title.   [DNLM: 1.   Emotions—
Popular works.   BF561 Y75u]
  BF531.Y63   152.4   75-31523
  ISBN 0-13-936518-4
  ISBN 0-13-936500-1 pbk.

© 1975 by Prentice-Hall, Inc., Englewood Cliffs, New Jersey

A Spectrum Book

10   9   8   7   6   5   4   3   2   1

Printed in the United States of America

Prentice-Hall International, Inc., *London*
Prentice-Hall of Australia Pty. Ltd., *Sydney*
Prentice-Hall of Canada, Ltd., *Toronto*
Prentice-Hall of India Private Limited, *New Delhi*
Prentice-Hall of Japan, Inc., *Tokyo*
Prentice-Hall of Southeast Asia (Pte.) Ltd., *Singapore*

Contents

3   FEELING AND KNOWING   31

Preface

The behavioral revolution of the twentieth century biased psychology toward a scientific, objective view of human nature. Consequently, individual, subjective conscious experiences, known in scientific terms as "affective" experiences, tended to be ignored and the introspective method fell into disrepute. Feelings, felt emotions, images, meanings, values, purposive intentions, and the like were held to be beyond the scope of natural science.

The time is ripe to consider human feelings and emotions in a new light. It is, of course, possible to hold to a consistent physical view of the universe and claim that all else is nonscience. But in such a light this book has no right to exist, for it is not consistently physical and objective. My outlook is interdisciplinary; it accepts the entire scientific view of the world at face value, but it also accepts the reality of subjective phenomena. For everything that you *are* and *do* depends upon the way you feel—and the way you look at things.

Feelings and emotions depend for their existence upon events inside your skin. They depend also upon external environmental conditions that are perceived or remembered or imagined. Emotions and feelings are manifested objectively in behavior and as internal bodily processes. They are also *felt* within a person, and they often lead to intentions to act in particular ways.

There is a vast difference between the approaches of the objective physical sciences, on the one hand, and the subjective, individual point of view, on the other. I have perceptions, sensations, conscious feelings and emotions, unconscious drives, memories, fantasies, frustrations, and persisting inner conflicts. I also have a sense of freedom of choice and a recognition of my responsibility for the consequences of choice. There is in me an awareness of right and wrong, of morality, religion, law and order. There are rewards and punishments. All these things depend upon my own unique conscious experience. When I am faced with the need to make an immediate "moral" decision, I do not think about my increased heartbeat, my sweaty palms, my lack of homeostasis. But in my calmer moments I often wonder how I can learn to control my anger, or learn to have more fun, or *feel* better.

There is a need for a sound psychology of conscious experience and unconscious motivation. We need to bring the diverse scientific and personal facts of human experience together so that we may find law and order in a universe that contains feelings, meanings, desires, values, intentions, and an array of related psychological (and physical) occurrences. We need a sensible and realistic approach to affective psychology.

This book is an attempt to present in an elementary, nontechnical way an understanding of our feelings and emotions—our affective processes. It is my attempt to organize the complex and controversial field of affective psychology as far as possible in the light of my own research and study. When we consider the many pressing social problems that confront humanity we realize the need for a sound view of human nature. Man is in part, but only in part, a rational animal. In the book I will try to bring together the knowledge of objective science and that of the subjective experience in an effort to better understand the nature and causes of emotion and feeling, how they work, and even what can be done about and with them. Hopefully, in spite of the differences in these two viewpoints, this will make possible a more complete and adequate account of the whole array of facts concerning human feelings and emotions.

For more than half a century I have investigated the nature and function of affective arousals. My early experiments, using an introspective method, were performed under the supervision of Edward Bradford Titchener. Subsequently I turned to behavioral experiments on the food preferences, appetites and dietary habits of the rat with a biological and physiological approach. My research has been published in a series of experimental and theoretical papers in technical journals and in several books. These studies have provided a factual basis for this book.

My obligations are many. Specific credit for illustrations and quotations has been given at the place of citation. I am indebted to the American Psychological Association for permission to reproduce figures published in copyrighted journal articles. I am indebted to Prentice-Hall, Inc., of Englewood Cliffs, New Jersey, for permission to reproduce several illustrations from my chapter entitled "Feeling and Emotion" in B. B. Wolman, ed., *Handbook of General Psychology* (1973). The Robert E. Krieger Publishing Company of Huntington, New York, has granted permission to republish several illustrations from the second revised edition of my *Emotion in Man and Animal: Its Nature and Dynamic Basis* (1973). John Wiley & Sons, Inc., of New York, have given permission to quote several paragraphs regarding stress from my

Motivation and Emotion: A Survey of the Determinants of Human and Animal Activity (1961).

During the early stages of writing this book Professor Arthur T. Jersild made helpful suggestions regarding the plan and outline of the content. Professor David F. Ricks read the completed manuscript and indicated ways in which it could be improved. His advice has been helpful during revision of the text. For competent help with typing the manuscript I am indebted to Thelma Kramar and Cheryl Dixon. I am especially grateful to Lynne A. Lumsden, Editor of Spectrum Books of Prentice-Hall, Inc., for her encouragement in the writing of this book and for constant assistance and supervision while seeing the work through the press. Finally, Mary M. Allen has gone over the entire text adding examples from her experience and greatly improving the readability and style.

1 The Way We Look at Things

AFFECT, AFFECTIVE, AFFECTION Having to do with feelings and emotions.

AFFECTIVE AROUSAL A temporary process of feeling (anger, embarrassment, fear), as distinct from a more permanent emotional state.

AFFECT-INDUCING SITUATION Sum total of environmental and/or organic conditions initiating feeling or emotion. Includes perceived events as well as memories, fantasies, and physiological conditions.

AFFECTIVE PSYCHOLOGY That branch of psychology which deals with feelings and emotions, as distinct from *cognitive psychology*.

ATTENTION SET Selective observation of a specific object or idea. Concentration.

COGNITION Knowing; awareness of meaning.

COGNITIVE ORGANIZATION (1) Integration of information or knowledge into a single belief, plan, or expectancy; or (2) unit of knowledge thus integrated.

COGNITIVE PSYCHOLOGY Deals with perceiving, remembering, thinking, and related mental processes, as distinct from *affective psychology*.

INTROSPECTION The process of observing and reporting conscious phenomena, whether sensory, affective, or cognitive.

MOODS Persistent affective states, less intense and less disruptive than emotions.

OBJECTIVE Related to something believed to exist independently of the observer.

PERCEPTION Observation of objects, events, and relations through the senses.

PERCEPTUAL FIELD Total area of sensory awareness at a given moment.

PHYSIOLOGICAL Referring to bodily functions of a living organism.

SENTIMENTS   Feelings determined by past experiences.

SUBJECTIVE   Related to conscious processes or awareness of a person who is the subject of experience. Subjective events can be defined by their dependence upon bodily, especially neural, events within the experiencing individual.

TEMPERAMENT   The relatively permanent affective traits that characterize a person.

Today everyone wants to know about his feelings and moods. Psychologists consider the individual person's observations about himself as well as the visible, provable scientific facts concerning emotions and feelings. It is now possible for people to find out about such things as depression, anxiety, pleasure, motivations, values. How often have you wondered why you feel and act the way you do? What is "being in love"? Why do you sometimes have bad moods? How did you learn to smile in the face of troubles? What does it mean when you feel guilty every time you lose your temper? Will it really help you understand your emotions to learn about measurable physical reactions to particular situations? And is it really possible that your description of the feeling in the pit of your stomach before an exam will help a scientist learn more about human emotions?

Recently, a cognitive psychology has arisen in protest to the overly scientific point of view which seemed to rely so heavily on observable, measurable factors that it forgot the very real, very important human being. True, you cannot open up the brain and find a specific area called "love," or "jealousy," or "loyalty." You cannot measure hate, or put guilt under a microscope. But surely your *knowledge*—your cognition—of how you feel is important in the total picture of human feelings. Cognitive psychology takes account of ideas and meanings. Cognitive meanings, however, can be distinguished from what the scientist calls "affective arousals." These are, in ordinary language, the very things that cause us to act and feel in particular ways. Meanings commonly fuse with feelings, but you and I can distinguish between the cognitive (thinking) and affective (feeling) aspects of experience. This book is an attempt to pool the resources of both the objective, scientific body of knowledge and the personal, individual, *subjective* mine of valuable information about our feelings and emotions. This is what we might call an *affective psychology*.

"I think, therefore I am":
The Miracle of Consciousness

When you open your eyes in the morning you observe a physical world. When you study biology or physics or chemistry you gain some understanding of the incredible universe in which we live. Physical, biological, and social sciences add to our knowledge and to the sense of mystery as well.

There is an important dimension of the world we see and hear, or interpret through a process of *perception*. We can also conceptualize the world by way of ideas, ranging from simple thoughts to ideas so abstract that only an Einstein could formulate and grasp them. This is the dimension of meaning, or *cognition*.

Closely associated with meanings are our feelings and emotions, ranging, for example, from a mild flutter of pleasure to ecstatic joy, from mild fear to immobilizing terror, from slight irritation to a towering rage. We might say that feelings and meanings are *subjective* as contrasted with the objective properties of the world which press upon our sense organs, or which we manipulate in our thoughts about tangible things.

All of this objective world with its external reality, its meaning of independent existence, seems to vanish when we lapse into dreamless sleep or pass into coma. Consciousness, awareness of the world we live in, is a miracle.

There are other dimensions of the world and reality that we also recognize. There is the unconscious, that mysterious, perhaps equally miraculous part of human life in which needs are determined, decisions are made, emotions are born. Everyone has this "inner self," and wants to know more about it. How much does it have to do with our feelings and emotions? How does it shape and influence the way we look at the world? The way we act? Perhaps in this area there are mysteries that will never be unraveled, because the inner self is different in every human being, and it cannot be cut open and examined. But by studying human emotions, their causes and effects, and their very existence, perhaps it is possible to better understand ourselves. In an important way, this search for understanding may help us lead richer, more fulfilling lives. And it may prepare the way for our children to live in a better world.

The way we look at things is determined by many factors, conscious and unconscious. Some of the results of the way we see things, our interpretation of them, are observable (you turn pale); some can only be explained or described by the individual (you feel faint). In this book we will be concerned with our feelings and our emotions—our *affective processes*. To begin, we should take a closer look at the subjective and objective views.

The Scientist and You:
Subjective and Objective Views

The world in which we live—including physical bodies, logical meanings, and feelings and emotions—seems not to exist while we are asleep or unconscious. My *subjective*, or individual world depends upon bodily processes, especially those in the brain, for its very existence. This dependence defines the subjective view of the world.

But the *objective* world, we believe, continues to exist whether we are aware of it or not, whether we are awake or asleep. Objective scientists view the world *as if* it existed in its own right, independently of human experience.

It has been said that the objective view of the world is a view with "man left out"; the subjective view is one with "man left in." But if we leave man out, we dehumanize the world. Conscious perceptions, meanings, feelings, and values depend upon the brains of human beings. We believe, however, that the products of human cultures—including arts and crafts, beliefs, morals, religion, etc.—have an objective, independent existence apart from any particular observer.

So the distinction between subjective and objective, though true in part, has limitations. I, and I alone, can experience the nature of the fear I feel at the approach of a snarling dog. This is a *subjective* experience. But a bystander who sees the dog (which may or may not scare him) can perceive visible signs of my fright. If he possessed, and nonchalantly applied laboratory instruments, he could detect many physiological reactions in me that are not visible to the naked eye. These would be *objective* measures. Actually, in daily life, we recognize both subjective and objective ways of dealing with the world of experience. Regardless of what we observe objectively, or detect with laboratory instruments, there are psychological attributes of feelings and emotions which only I can be aware of as distinct personal experiences. And there are also attributes that exist that I am not aware of.

We recognize this in everyday life. A physician, trying to diagnose a disorder, asks about your symptoms. He wants to know how you feel. What pains, aches, chills, and other discomforts can you describe? At the same time he pays close attention to the objective signs of your illness. He takes your temperature, checks your swollen glands. Thus he relies upon observations from both points of view, subjective and objective.

Now if a physiologist, an objective scientist, observes directly the electrophysiological processes of the brain, he does not find love, hate, fear, anger, or any other feeling and emotion. But he can observe laughing, weeping, growling, fighting, fleeing, and other bits of emotional behavior. And he has found a physical basis for such things as wakefulness and sleep, pleasure and unpleasure, cognitive awareness, intentions to act and other realities of conscious existence. These dynamic processes involve a relation between an organism and its environment. They are observed objectively. And they must be considered relative to perceptions, sensations, feelings, emotions, values, intentions, and the like.

To describe emotional behavior and conscious experience completely we must consider the total situation, of which the brain is a part. And we must rely upon observations and reports from both the subjective and objective points of view. We may, if we wish, *infer* conscious feelings and emotions in other persons and animals. For example, you infer a state of pleasure when your dog wags his tail. But the pleasure is not observed directly in the animal's behavior nor in his brain. Objectively, pleasure is an inference.

How We Perceive Things

Perception is the primary and basic form of cognition. Remembering, thinking, and imagining are also cognitive processes. They rest upon perception. It is important, therefore, to examine the nature of perceiving.

In the simplest terms, to perceive is to observe through the senses. The model for perceiving is as follows:

$$\text{To perceive} = \begin{cases} \text{to see} \\ \text{to hear} \\ \text{to touch} \\ \text{to taste} \\ \text{to smell} \\ \text{to sense} \\ \quad \text{internally} \end{cases} \text{some} \begin{cases} \text{thing} \\ \text{event} \\ \text{relation} \end{cases}$$

Many examples of perceiving are found on every hand. When you say, "I see a red light," you are reporting something you are observing, or perceiving.

In every instance of perceiving there are several fundamental aspects. First, there is the *experiencing individual*. In the report "I see a red light," the "I" implies a subject of experience, an experiencing individual. Second, there is the *object* of perception—the thing, event, or relation that is observed. The object of perception is technically designated as the *percept*. The report, "a red light," indicates a particular sensory quality that has form and meaning. The percept may be a physical body, a melody, a pleasant fragrance, an accident, or a relation such as "heavier than" or "to the left of." Third, perceiving is a *process*. It is this aspect that presents to the psychologist a number of fundamental and central problems.

Behind every act of perceiving is the individual's past history and experience. Previous experience has built up a relatively stable *cognitive organization* (knowledge, expectancy) within the individual which determines the meaning of a particular percept.

To the psychologist the importance of perceiving lies in the fact that it is related to every aspect of mental activity. Perceiving is related to action—you see a red light and step on your brakes. Perceiving is related to memory—you recognize the face of a friend in a crowd. Perceiving is related to the arousal of emotion—you see a picture of a swastika. Perceiving is related to thinking—when you read a problem and start to work out a solution, your reasoning is initiated by the perception of printed words. Perceiving is also related to motivation—you are out of cigarettes and see them on a counter, so you buy a pack. The want was there, of course, but in this case perception triggered the action.

Perceiving, in fact, enters into all aspects of our lives, conscious and unconscious, including our feelings and emotions.

Paying Attention: The Selective Organization of Attention

When you are paying attention to a particular object, event, or relation, that thing—the percept—stands out clearly in your consciousness. Surrounding objects and events in your perceptual field are less clear, less prominent. Parts of your surroundings which you know are there (what is behind your head, for example) are not present in your perceptual awareness. (You are not *conscious* of them.) The process of attending is selective. Attending brings into focus certain parts of your surroundings. It makes them more clear and vivid, and it blocks out (inhibits) other parts.

The objective scientist would say that attention involves the facilitation of some neural excitations and the inhibition of others. Perhaps you would say, "All I saw was the blood—I didn't even notice the man with the knife running away."

Attention organizes your experience in space and time, giving form to the percept. It causes a mental "set"—an *attention set*. To illustrate, consider Figure 1.

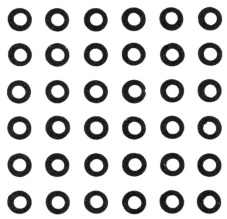

Figure 1. A figure to demonstrate how perceptual groupings depend upon mental set. Slightly modified from Schumann (1900).

Assume that these circles are arranged in groups of four with spaces between them. Then look fixedly at the circles. They appear to be grouped into nine groups, four circles in each group. Now assume that they are grouped by nines; they *are* in groups of nines. Again, assume a grouping by sixes first in a horizontal and then in a vertical arrangement; the various groupings appear. A wide variety of patterns can be perceived merely by persistently looking at the figure with a particular mental set. Practice makes this observation more striking and easy.

Similarly, the attention set can organize (within limits) the sequence of events in time. There is a principle of attention known as the law of prior entry. Simply stated, it means that when two stimulations are physically simultaneous, the sensory impression you pay attention to is the first to enter your conscious awareness.

I discovered accidentally a simple way to demonstrate the law of prior entry. This way requires a little patience but none of the usual laboratory apparatus.

> Lie down and relax. With your left hand, feel your pulse just in front of the left ear, and with your right hand feel the pulse in front of the right ear. Attending to the two pulses, you will perceive them to be simultaneous. Now by concentrating on the left pulse, you can perceive the sequence: lr, lr, lr. . . . Then by concentrating on the right pulse, perceive the sequence: rl, rl, rl. . . . The temporal order that you perceive depends upon the set of attention.

The attention set or sharp concentration can be a factor in the observation of events which are simultaneous or nearly so. For example, in a baseball game the runner slides to third base at the same time the ball plops into the glove of the third baseman. The umpire says, *"Out!"* The manager of the team rushes forward and protests that the player is *safe.* The sequence of events has differed for each observer. From one point of view the runner is out, from another, he is safe.

The attention set, obviously, has a lot to do with how we see the world. It is also important in most studies of how and what people feel.

The Nature of Feeling: The Kinds and Sources of Affectivity

The affective processes, which by now we know concern our feelings, are the ways things affect *you.* They can be described either subjectively or objectively. We can say that a Hitchcock movie makes us excited, horrified, frightened; or we can say that the suspense in that movie made our hair stand on end, our hands tremble, and our mouths dry. There are several varieties of affective processes:

Sense feelings come from the stimulations of the sense organs. Such stimulation can originate in the environment or within the body. Pleasant feelings, for example, can result from *hearing* a beautiful flute solo. Smelling sulphur is an unpleasant sense feeling. There are also internal sense feelings of comfort (positive) and discomfort (negative).

Emotions are complex affective processes and states that originate in the situations of life a person has to cope with. They manifest themselves in subjective feelings—sadness, joy, terror. Emotions can be caused by painful stimulation, frustration, conflict, or the release of tension. The words "I forgive you, darling" can bring about relief in an emotion that may show itself in either laughter or tears.

I have elsewhere defined emotion as a *disturbed* affective state that originates in the psychological situation. Although disturbances are usually thought of as unpleasant, there are *positive* emotions of joy, laughter, ecstasy, etc., that are, in fact, acutely disorganized emotional states.

The concept of emotion applies not only to the immediate outburst or upset which you feel and observe but also to persisting mental states such as anxiety, hostility, love, humiliation, and the like.

Moods are persistent mental states which are less intense and less disruptive than emotions. There are moods of cheerfulness, depression, excitement, resentment, and so forth.

Activity feelings are associated with feelings of interest or disinterest. For example, you may love to play tennis, in fact are ready any time to play a set. But if someone suggests an early-morning sail, you may not be interested—because you are disinclined to get wet and chilly, for you have no skill in sailing. We speak of this as an *aversion* to something, while the opposite would be described as an *appetitive* state ("She has a fantastic appetite for skiing"). Activity feelings also include the urge to action motivated by such organic states as hunger, thirst, the need to eliminate, sexual needs, etc.

Sentiments are affective processes based on past experiences: memories of places, situations, persons, etc. Sentimental feelings are elicited by words, odors, pictures, and other sensory clues that re-arouse latent feelings. You may forever associate the smell of Chanel No. 5 with your first dinner date, which was a disaster—you'll feel that same dreadful feeling again every time you catch a whiff of that perfume. Sentiments are meaningful experiences, somewhat akin to moods.

Temperament refers to relatively permanent affective dispositions and traits that characterize the person as a whole. Frank is always bouncy and cheerful; Laura seems to maintain an air of gloomy pessimism.

The word *affect* is one we will see often in a text concerning the emotions and feelings of human beings. It is commonly used to designate normal affective processes. However, we should be aware that in psychiatry the term is also used to describe intense pathological affective states. Thus a deep depression, an excited euphoria, an acute feeling of personal guilt, a complete apathy, and so forth are sometimes called *affects*.

In the chapters that follow, we will attempt to gain an understanding of the nature and causes of feelings and emotions. What is their role in human life? How can they be controlled? How are they important in understanding our changing world? How will knowing more about our feelings help us live better lives? Make this a better world? The facts about feelings and emotions are complex and controversial. We will examine them in the light of contemporary research, hopefully relating such study to our own lives.

2 Your Emotions and Moods

ADAPTIVE BEHAVIOR   Activity that shows a tendency to fit a particular situation, often by modifying a pre-existing situation.

BEHAVIORISM   A doctrine that the data of psychology consist solely of observable evidences of organic activity, to the exclusion of introspective data or references to consciousness or mind.

CEREBRAL   Related to the cerebrum or brain. The cortex, or outer layer, of the brain is believed to be essential to intellect and complex mental processes.

CONTINUUM   Something absolutely continuous, an unbroken variable as a line generated by a moving point.

BIPOLAR CONTINUUM   A continuous variable between opposite poles, such as that between pleasure and unpleasure. (Indifference is actually a middle range along this continuum rather than an ideal zero point.)

HEDONIC   Related to and characterized by pleasure and its opposite, unpleasure.

INNATE   Inborn.

INTEGRATION   Coordination.

PSYCHOLOGICAL INTEGRATION   The coordination of processes or states into a unit of personality or mental activity.

NEURAL INTEGRATION   The coordination of neural parts in a unitary reaction. (The simplest movement of a leg or arm is controlled by antagonistic pairs of muscles that are simultaneously excited and inhibited in a reciprocal relation by nerve centers within the central nervous system.)

NONAFFECTIVE STATE   A conscious condition that is free from feelings and emotions.

NONEMOTIONAL NORM   An undisturbed affective state that is estimated to be somewhere between complete integration (organization) and maximal disorganization. The nonemotional norm differs from person to person.

PURPOSIVE BEHAVIOR   Activity that is oriented toward or against a specific goal, terminal state, or end.

Everyone, except perhaps the psychologist, knows what an emotion is. Terror, rage, horror, embarrassment, excitement, disgust, grief, jealousy, shame, amusement, ecstasy, sorrow—all these *are* emotions. You have no problem identifying most emotions. You know it is anger you feel when someone bashes your fender in a parking lot and leaves without so much as an apology. The problem for the psychologist is that emotions are extremely complex. They must be analyzed from various points of view and in relation to almost everything else with which he deals.

Today it is not enough for most people to merely know that they *have* emotions. They want to know *why* they have them, and what to do about some of them. Why am I so depressed when everything seems to be going well? Why is Bob afraid of heights? Why does Alex ruin every romantic relationship with unreasonable jealousy? The psychologist's and the layman's interest in such problems overlaps. In such an atmosphere it is possible for those who make a study of human emotions to help people gain a practical insight into their emotions.

History of the Word *Emotion*

According to Murray's (1888) dictionary, the word *emotion* is derived from the Latin *e* (out) and *movere* (to move). Originally the word meant a moving out of one place to another, in the sense of a migration. Thus: "The divers emotions of that people [the Turks]" (1603). "Some accidental Emotion . . . of the Center of Gravity" (1695). The word came to mean a moving, stirring, or agitation in a strictly physical sense. Thus: "Thunder . . . caused so great an Emotion in the air" (1708). This physical meaning was gradually transferred to political and social agitation; the word came to mean tumult, popular disturbance. Thus: "There were . . . great stirres and emocions in Lombardy" (1579). Finally the word came to be used to designate any agitated, vehement, or excited mental state of the individual. Thus: "The joy of gratification is properly called an emotion" (1762).

Aristotle (384–322 B.C.) used the word *passion* (παθη) to include appetite, anger, fear, confidence, envy, joy, love, hate, longing, emulation, pity, and in general, various states accompanied by pleasure and pain. Incidentally, this Greek root appears in words that describe some illnesses and physical disturbances (*pathology*) as well as conscious feelings (*sympathy, empathy, apathy*). The passions were roughly equivalent to what psychologists today call *affective processes.*

Ludovicus Vives (1492–1540), however, used the term *passiones* as appropriate only to violent emotions. Thus rage, terror, horror, agony, and ecstasy were among the passions. The modern word *emotion* is sometimes used in Aristotle's sense to include the whole gamut of affective processes and sometimes in the more restricted sense of Vives to designate affective processes that are intense, disruptive, disorganized, violent. (See Gardiner, Metcalf, and Beebe-Center, 1937, pp. 42, 123.)

RECOGNIZING AND NAMING EMOTIONS

Today there are many words in the English language that designate feelings, emotions, and attitudes. Kanner, in his 1931 study, projected upon a screen a series of facial expressions of human emotions. Students in six classes were instructed to write "the best" descriptive term for each facial expression. Ignoring duplicates, Kanner found that the students had used 365 terms. Obviously, that doesn't mean there are 365 human emotions! It does mean that there are many words to describe each emotion and, perhaps more importantly, many ways of *perceiving* expressions of emotions. One facial expression may look like more than one emotion. For example, an expression of fear may look much the same as one of surprise. Aunt Phoebe, peeking at the baby in the carriage, may exhibit the same open mouth, wide eyes, raised brows that would indicate her fear at seeing a mouse.

We can see that there is a problem in distinguishing and interpreting different forms of emotion. How can specific emotions be recognized and named?

Facial Expressions

How accurately can we recognize emotions by facial expressions? In an early study Landis (1924) aroused genuine emotions under laboratory conditions. He photographed the face and studied the records in the hope of finding specific *patterns* of emotional expression.

To evoke genuine emotions Landis employed such situations as listening to music, smelling ammonia, writing out a *faux pas,* reading pornographic material, handling live frogs, experiencing electric shocks, and, finally, relief from these various ordeals.

Dark marks were placed on the subject's face and then measured on photographs to show the degree to which different groups of facial muscles were contracted in emotional states and at rest. The subjects also gave verbal reports of their emotional experiences.

As a result of his experiment, Landis made certain generalizations. Apparently there are wide individual differences in facial expressions. In this study, there was no fixed expression common to any single situation. Moreover, everyone tends to use some particular group of facial muscles habitually. This means that we all have certain characteristic facial patterns. It was also found that in the case of imagined emotions, there seems to be no uniform facial expression.

On the basis of these and other generalizations, Landis concluded that an emotion, as it is observed in the face, is not a true pattern of response as is, for example, the wink reflex. He suggested that the common names of emotions typically refer to the *situations* which induce them rather than to the patterns of facial responses.

Landis believed that *posed* expressions are conventional and that they are used for communication much as are spoken words. These conventional expressions differ from culture to culture. Thus he thought of emotional expression as being both social (learned) and reflexive, or biologically basic. When you gasp and recoil at the sight of a large spider you are showing an instinctive expression of emotion. When you smile as you are being introduced in a reception line (even though you want to go home and take your shoes off), you are showing a social expression.

But we all know, that some emotional reactions can be readily identified and named from facial expressions. Izard (1971) made cross-cultural studies of facial expressions and found basic uniformities. Some facial expressions are biologically innate. See, for example, the facial expressions of crying and laughing in the infant, Figure 2. These expressions of distress and delight are universally recognized. Their names, of course, vary from language to language.

Hebb (1946) made an interesting study of the emotional behavior of the chimpanzee—man's closest primate relative. He examined the diary records kept for thirty chimpanzees to discover how emotions were recognized and named by persons who had cared for the animals for long periods of time. Hebb concluded that temperamental traits and specific emotions are recognized primarily as *deviations from normal behavior.*

 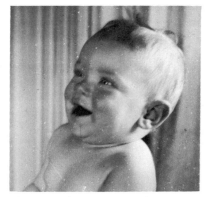

Figure 2. Crying and laughing in the infant. Courtesy of Dr. Nancy Bayley.

Perhaps it would help to think of normal behavior as that behavior most people exhibit in their attempts to stay *balanced.* This means that most people have a desire to maintain some sort of equilibrium in their lives. Although excitement is sought out, and some change is often welcomed, most people we consider to be emotionally healthy— that is, well-adjusted individuals—prefer to have some degree of predictability in their lives. In this quest for balance, most people like to have their meals regularly, to sleep every night, find that being paid regularly for their work makes them feel secure and reasonably happy. And so forth. In establishing these habits, in searching for integration and meaning and regularity, most human beings establish some sort of routine. It may be a "kooky" routine, according to the standards of others, but there is some pattern to it. And when the man down the street, who has come home from work carrying his umbrella and his evening paper at promptly 5:15 every Monday to Friday for twelve years, is seen in mid-afternoon on a red motorcycle going down the wrong side of the road, this would easily be recognized as a deviation from his normal behavior base.

To return to Hebb's study: Chimpanzees, like human beings, form habits of expression and have well-marked individual differences in emotional behavior. Hebb concluded that the observer's interpretation of facial expression depends upon both a knowledge of the subject and an understanding of the situation that caused the emotion. You may be the only person in the room who knows that the wide smile on your friend's face means not that he is happy, but that he is about to burst with impatience and boredom.

What Makes You Do Things: The Inducing Situation

The importance of understanding the emotion-inducing situation in naming emotions was shown in a study by Schachter and Singer (1962). They injected people in their experiment with epinephrine. This drug produces tremor, increases the rate and strength of the heartbeat, accelerates breathing, and causes other observable bodily symptoms. They also controlled the subject's *understanding* of the experimental situation. Some subjects were given correct information about the physiological effects of the drug, some were given 'no information. Others were intentionally misinformed: "Your feet will feel numb, you will have an itching sensation over parts of your body, and you may get a slight headache."

After injection, each subject was approached by a "stooge," who acted either in a euphoric or in an angry manner. The social environment was thus varied and controlled. Emotional behavior was rated by both the people who were taking part in the study and hidden observers.

Schachter and Singer concluded that both the physiological state and the understanding of the situation influence a person's ability to name emotions. Under the same drug-induced bodily state, a subject labeled his emotion as "joy" or "anger" according to his understanding of the inducing situation. Further, it was seen that if an individual had no immediate explanation for his bodily state, he described his feelings in terms of whatever knowledge he had. From this study we can see that our understanding of the situation—whether it is correct or not—plays an important role in recognizing and naming emotions. This is true for naming the emotions of others as well as interpreting our own. (See also Hunt, Cole, and Reis, 1958.)

Why You Respond: The Effect of Stimulation

Tolman (1923) emphasized the importance of a person's reaction to the emotion-causing situation in a behavioristic account of emotions. It is not the stimulus situation *as such* that helps us define emotions. Rather it is our *response* to the situation as we deal—or try to deal—with it. Thus, in fear it is escape (a toddler runs away from a loud noise). In anger it is destruction (a man smashes his fist through the window that refuses to budge). And in love it is encouragement or enticement (a mother caresses her child). These are the sorts of action which objectively characterize specific emotions. According to Tolman, each emotion is characterized by a tendency toward its own particular type of adaptive behavior. Thus an emotion has motivation effectiveness; *it leads to purposive behavior.*

I will add that purposive, goal-oriented behavior is often the outcome of emotional disturbance. An emotional problem may be solved by a change of goal or attitude. We will have more to say about this later.

BRIEF HISTORY OF THEORIES OF EMOTIONS AND FEELINGS

The modern period began with the work of Darwin (1872) on *the expression of the emotions in man and animals.* Darwin gave an evolutionary interpretation to emotional reactions. The overt signs of emotion, he argued, are related to the life-and-death struggle for survival and to reproduction of the species. Some emotional expressions, however, lack the obvious biological utility—such emotions as weeping and laughing. Useless expressions must be explained in terms of the constitution of the nervous system.

William James' paper "What Is an Emotion?" appeared in *Mind* in 1884. He regarded emotion as a *conscious experience characterized by the awareness of bodily changes.* His striking statement raised a philosophical discussion of the perennial mind-body relation. The James-Lange theory inspired the physiological research of Walter B. Cannon, and others.

The first laboratory of experimental psychology was founded by Wilhelm Wundt in Leipzig, 1879. Through introspective studies of the senses and experiments on simple affective processes, Wundt formulated a tridimensional theory of feeling (see page 26) which influenced research during the period between 1880 and 1920.

Wundt's pupil, E. B. Titchener, continued the introspective tradition in America. Titchener reduced Wundt's three affective dimensions to one: pleasantness and unpleasantness. Later in his career Titchener came to regard the affective processes as sensory in nature. (See the study by Henle, 1974.)

At the turn of the century, in Europe and America, there was considerable research with the so-called *expressive* methods. It was widely recognized that conscious feelings and emotions are outwardly "expressed" in bodily changes and behavior. Experimental studies of pleasantness and unpleasantness sought to find correlations between these subjective feelings and their physiological manifestations. Studies were made of peripheral bodily changes in pulse, blood pressure, respiration, electrical changes at the surface of the body, involuntary movements, and other peripheral processes.

Some correlations were found. For example, reports of pleasantness correlated with vasodilation and unpleasantness with vasoconstriction, but the correlations were not perfect. There was no *sine qua non* of the simple feelings. Failure of the expressive methods was blamed (perhaps unfairly) on the introspective technique. We know now that the physiological basis of emotional processes lies deeply buried in the central nervous system. Possibly there are no signs of positive and negative feelings that always occur at the surface of the body.

Beginning about 1914, came the behavioral revolution, led by John B. Watson and subsequently advanced through the years by B. F. Skinner. Watson defined emotion as a behavioral pattern that involves the muscles and glands. His theory outlawed the introspective method, with the result (as we have seen) that the study of subjective feelings (and images) came to be regarded as scientifically taboo.

During the early decades of this century, the work of Cannon, Bard, and other physiologists was centered on the bodily basis of emotional reactions. Emphasis was shifted from exterior bodily changes to the autonomic nervous system and subsequently to the neural basis of affective processes within the central nervous system. (In Chapter 4 we will discuss some of the physiological theories at greater length.)

In 1951, Donald B. Lindsley published a paper on emotion in which he reviewed experimental research and presented a theory of excited emotions based on the functions of what is called the reticular activating system. (See page 57.) Lindsley's theory provided a sound physiological basis for a theory of drive as a diffuse general motivation.

In 1954, James Olds with P. Milner published a paper on positive reinforcement produced by electical stimulation of a particular area of the rat brain. In the same year, J. M. R. Delgado, W. W. Roberts, and N. E. Miller published an account of learning motivated by electrical stimulation of the cat brain.

These and subsequent studies provided a sound basis for the hypothesis of diffuse, nonspecific, positive and negative arousals during feelings and emotions. This kind of physiological basis is implied in the psychophysical studies of food preferences of rats, reported by Paul T. Young, and others, during the early 1960s. (See Young, 1967a and 1967b.)

Historically viewed, there has been a transition from a speculative and introspective view of feelings and emotions to objective and behavioral accounts. And, further, there is now a view that takes account of both the subjective and objective data that relate to affective processes.

There has also been a change from study of peripheral (exterior) bodily processes regulated by the autonomic nervous system to investigation of central neural and chemical processes. Present emphasis is on the neurochemical processes located deeply in the brain stem and cerebrum, as we will discuss in a later chapter.

Finally, there has been a transition from the study of specific patterns of affective reaction to a more comprehensive view of total behavior. The latter view takes account of man's perceptions, memories, fantasies, and total cognitive processes, as man copes with emotional problems that arise in his environment and persist through time.

DARWIN'S PRINCIPLES OF EMOTIONAL EXPRESSION

When we talk about "expression" of emotion we are referring to behavior that can be seen and heard. The term implies a central process that is outwardly "expressed." This central process may be conceived as a conscious experience or as an electrochemical event in the brain.

This concern with emotional expression is not new. Over a hundred years ago Darwin (1872) published a work entitled *The Expression of Emotions in Man and Animal,* in which he gave an evolutionary interpretation of emotional behavior. The work brought together a mass of accurate scientific observations and some personal interpretation relating to emotional reactions. It was probably the most influential book on the subject during the nineteenth century.

Darwin interpreted emotional behavior in terms of three principles. The first, which he called *serviceable associated habits,* states that emotional expressions are associated with behavior that has biological utility in the struggle for existence and in preservation of the species. Thus when an angry man bares his teeth by curling his lips he probably does not really intend to bite, but the expression is a vestige of a biologically useful act. (However, it might be mentioned parenthetically that in a fracas that is recognized by the participants to be a "fight to the finish," even the most "civilized" person may be reduced to using every means at his disposal to win—including actual biting!) The emotional behavior of animals in the wild has obvious utility in defense against predators, attack of prey, mating, care of the young, and related biological activities.

Consider, for example, the behavior of the hostile cat, Figure 3 *a.* This animal is ready to spring and attack an enemy. The tip of the tail

Figure 3. Emotional expressions of the cat. *(a)* Hostile cat prepared for attack. *(b)* Friendly, pleasant, cat. *(c)* Cat terrified by a barking dog. *Redrawn by* Mrs. K. H. Paul from Darwin (1872).

is lashed or curled from side to side; the hair, especially on the tail, bristles; the ears are pressed backward into a position that protects them during a fight; the mouth is open, teeth bared; the forefeet are ready to strike, with claws protruding; the animal growls.

Now by way of contrast, look at the posture and behavior of the friendly cat, Figure 3 *b*. This illustrates Darwin's second principle, the *principle of antithesis*. Instead of crouching for attack, the friendly cat stands erect with back slightly arched; the tail is rigid and stands straight up; the hair is smooth; the ears are erect and pointed; the mouth is closed and relaxed; the claws are withdrawn; instead of a growl the vocalization is a purr. The friendly cat rubs against the leg of her master. In a word, friendly behavior is the complete opposite of hostile behavior. Friendly behavior expresses the biological meaning: I am *not* your enemy.

Consider now the expression of terror, Figure 3 *c*. This figure shows the reaction of a cat to a barking dog. This expression is more akin to pure hostility than to friendliness. As in hostility the hair bristles; the pupils are dilated; the ears are pressed back; the teeth are bared; the claws protrude; the back is arched; the animal hisses, perhaps as a warning to her enemy. The terrified cat is poised so that either attack or flight is possible. The animal can turn and run for a tree, or, if cornered, fight. The behavior has utility in the struggle for existence.

Darwin recognized that the first two principles do not alone explain all the natural expressions of emotion. So he formulated a third principle. Some expressions, he argued, must be explained in terms of the *direct action of the nervous system*. Thus, such behavior as writhing in agony or screaming or laughing during emotional excitement must be interpreted in terms of neural function. Here there is no obvious utility for survival.

Darwin believed that there is an overflow of nervous excitations in highly excited emotional states. This overflow produces physiological changes that are outwardly expressed quite apart from the principles of biological utility and antithesis. This third principle has been exceedingly useful in the modern studies of the physiological (neural and chemical) changes that occur during emotion.

One final point should be made. Behavior that has no survival value for the individual may still have survival value for the species. Thus when the hen sights a hawk overhead, she utters a sound of alarm that causes her chicks to scamper for shelter. And when the young of many species cry, if hungry, the signal causes the mother to feed them or to retrieve them if they have wandered from the nest. Such social behavior has obvious biological utility.

HOW FEELINGS AND EMOTIONS VARY: DIMENSIONS OF AFFECTIVE AROUSAL

If emotions are recognized as deviations from normal behavior, as Hebb thought, it is important to discover and describe the normal "nonemotional" condition. What is the most nonemotional condition that you can imagine?

Some will think of sleep as a nonemotional condition. Sleep is a kind of zero point for all conscious experiences. But what about sexual and other emotional dreams? Do you recall ever having had such a terrifying nightmare that you woke up breathing hard? Or such a sad dream that you awoke to find tears on your face?

Some will think that the nonemotional norm is a routine, automatic, habitual pattern of activity such as passively twiddling the thumbs. In daily life there are many kinds of activity that are relatively free from feeling. Such experiences may approximate the nonemotional norm.

In Chapter 1 I defined emotion as a *disturbed* affective process or state that originates in a psychological situation. If a person were completely free from affective disturbance, he would be nonemotional.

In daily life we recognize disturbances that are affective and at the same time nonemotional. For example, if you are watching a TV program when the phone rings, you are disturbed—you go to the phone. In a sense, every distraction of attention is a disturbance but we do not usually regard minor distractions as emotional.

It is important to realize that there are degrees of emotional disturbance. In one family of emotions the affective intensity varies from mild annoyance to moderate anger to a towering rage. In another family there are gradations from mild apprehension to moderate fright to disruptive terror. In still another family there are differences of emotional intensity from mild joy through various degrees of euphoria to ecstasy.

Any distinction between emotional and nonemotional states must be arbitrary. There are varying degrees of affective disorganization (or organization). The definition of emotion as a *disturbed* affective state is controversial. Although almost all psychologists admit the existence of emotional upset, some point out that emotions are organizing, integrating factors in human life. Consider, for example, the case of a man at a religious revival. He is remorseful over his evil life and sins; he has intense guilt feelings. He is converted and becomes committed to leading a better life. Now instead of remorse there is joy and a positive, organized outlook on life. Or consider the citizen who reads about atrocities of the enemy. He understands that the enemy is planning to invade his land and destroy his home. He is emotionally upset. He hears an appeal to join the army; his emotional disturbance may lead to a commitment and thus a reorganization of his plan of life.

Emotional disturbance is a fact of life. But we can see that such disturbances can be healthy. They often lead to behavioral organization and integration. Emotional disorganization actually causes the formation of motives and attitudes, as well as the development of traits of personality.

This matter of emotional organization and disorganization will be considered in a later chapter when we discuss emotional development. (See page 89.) In the meantime it may help to clarify the picture if we consider the hypothetical dimensions along which emotions vary.

The Activity Dimension

Lindsley (1951) thought of emotion as a highly excited state of the organism. He formulated a physiological theory of excited emotion and motivation.

In this theory, Lindsley represented different levels of activation on a linear continuum (Figure 4). In great states of excitement we may only be aware of certain elements in the critical situation. Or our awareness may be divided when there is confusion and haziness. During a less excited state we may be alert and attentive. Our concentration is focused. (We referred to this as *attention set* in Chapter 1.) There is also a relaxed state of wakefulness, when attention easily wanders. This state favors free association. You may have experienced this state in daydreaming. Drowsiness is a borderline condition with partial awareness. Then there is reverie and a dreamlike consciousness. In light sleep there is some loss of consciousness; but dreams may occur and be remembered. On the levels of deep sleep, coma, and death, there is, of course, a complete loss of awareness.

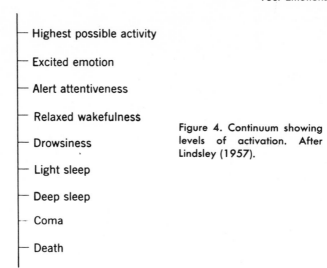

Highest possible activity

Excited emotion

Alert attentiveness

Relaxed wakefulness

Drowsiness

Light sleep

Deep sleep

Coma

Death

Figure 4. Continuum showing levels of activation. After Lindsley (1957).

This continuum of levels of activation corresponds closely to the continuum of activity in the sphere of behavior. There are highly excited states and states of calm and relaxation. Undifferentiated excitement has often been described as the primary emotional state.

The nonemotional norm probably belongs somewhere near the middle of this continuum. In considering normal emotions, we are concerned with conscious awareness and behavior, rather than with lower levels of unconscious activity.

The Pleasure Dimension

The linear continuum of activation has obvious limitations. It does not distinguish specific forms of emotional excitement. It disregards the depressed emotional states of sadness, grief, and discouragement. It also does not distinguish between the positive (pleasant) and the negative (unpleasant) affective states.

Thus a second dimension of emotional arousal must be added—the *hedonic dimension,* Figure 5. (*Hedonic* simply implies pleasure.) The hedonic continuum extends from maximal distress at the negative pole through a wide range of indifferent experiences to maximal delight at the positive pole. Arrows indicate two important directions of hedonic change: change away from the negative toward the positive pole; and change away from the positive toward the negative pole.

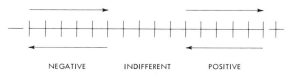

Figure 5. The bipolar hedonic continuum showing wide indifferent range and four directions of hedonic change. Modified from Beebe–Center (1932).

Pleasant and unpleasant experiences are produced by both simple and complex sensory stimulations. They are also produced by cognitive experiences such as good or bad news, victory or defeat, success or failure in an undertaking. They can even be produced by direct stimulation in certain areas of the subcortical neural structures. (See page 59.) Indeed, positive and negative affective arousals are elicited by many conditions.

Pleasant emotional experiences may occur at high levels of activation as in joy, uproarious laughter, ecstasy. They occur also at low levels of arousal, as in feelings of satisfaction, comfort, and relaxed enjoyment. Unpleasant experiences also occur at high levels of activation as in agony, unpleasant excitement, and at low levels of arousal as in feelings of disappointment, discouragement, discomfort, and the like.

The hedonic continuum (Figure 5) shows a wide range of indifferent arousals midway between the positive and negative poles. This range represents experiences and reactions that are only mildly positive or mildly negative. Arousals within this range are characterized by the level of activity and excitement that is felt and shown in behavior. For example, there are many types of behavior that indicate caution and curiosity. They are called hedonically "neutral." Complete neutrality, as indicated above, is only a hypothetical condition that we rarely if ever realize in daily life. But neutrality may be sought as a goal. For example, the Hindu mystics seek nirvana—a place or state of oblivion to care, pain, or external reality. They strive to reach nirvana through meditation or yoga. Peace of mind becomes a goal of life in the Hindu religion.

The Integration Dimension

The activity dimension and the pleasure dimension of emotional arousal are not enough to describe the varying degrees of emotional expression. A third dimension is needed. This is the dimension of *total integration.* It implies complete mental (cerebral) control of behavior at one extreme, and disorganization of planned and purposive behavior with weakening or loss of mental control at the other. This concept is basic for any definition of emotion.

It is easy to see the contrast between organized and disorganized activity. Disorganized activity is confused, nonspecific. Picture a mother trying to fix peanut butter sandwiches, hold a squirming baby, and answer the phone all at once. She may understandably look frantic and become increasingly disorganized in her activity!

Emotional—affective—reactions differ in the *degree of cerebral control* that is implied. Some highly motivated experiences can be well-integrated, purposive, and controlled. An airplane pilot, for example, may act in a controlled, integrated manner when his plane is in a tailspin. At the opposite extreme of this continuum, a frustrated individual may go berserk, become crazed, frenzied, with complete lack of control. Some pathological states are like this. In some psychoses the individual is not responsible for his actions.

In the definition of emotion as a disturbed (positive or negative) affective process or state with a psychological origin, a psychological event can be seen as more or less emotional, more or less organized or disorganized. Apart from acute emotional disturbances, there are chronic states of disorganization, such as anxiety, hostility, grief, that reveal themselves repeatedly in emotional outbreaks. Any account of emotion must consider these persisting states of affective disorganization.

The Stress Dimension

Other dimensions of emotional arousal have been proposed. In Wundt's classical three-dimensional theory of feeling there were three major parts: (1) excitement–calm, (2) pleasantness–unpleasantness, and (3) strain–relaxation. Wundt was considering simple feelings in proposing his theory, not complex emotional disruptions. Strain, he argued, is experienced when we expect or anticipate some event such as the click of a metronome; after the event there is relaxation.

The concept of anxiety tension or stress, as proposed by Selye (1956), is very much broader than Wundt's idea of strain. Selye's theory holds that such things as persisting cold, hunger, fatigue, loss of sleep, disease, threat, and other conditions produce stress. These same conditions *predispose* a person toward emotional outbreaks but do not necessarily *cause* emotional reactions. Emotional upsets are occasional events.

There are persisting states of emotional disorganization, such as lasting states of anxiety, tension, hostility, threat of some impending harm, bereavement, and the like. These mental states have a marked affective tone and they are practically important from the point of view of emotional health. Hence, when you view emotion as a condition that persists through time, the *level* of tension (strain or stress) is an important variable.

It should be pointed out, however, that from a clinical point of view anxiety covers much more than a concern over emotional problems of living. There are unconscious elements in anxiety states. And there are also such physical elements as glandular changes. (For a discussion of fear and anxiety, see p. 134.)

The Social Orientation Dimension

In an important study of moods, Nowlis and Nowlis (1956) suggested four dimensions of affectivity: (1) the activity dimension, (2) the pleasure dimension, (3) the level of control, and (4) social orientation. The first three of these dimensions have been considered above, but how about social orientation?

A person may be positively oriented toward others, or antisocial in his attitude—negatively oriented. We all know one or two "loners" who seem to prefer their own pursuits and activities to being in groups. An antisocial individual may actually seem self-centered and not at all concerned with the welfare of others. Other people are friendly, cooperative, and enjoy being with others. Thus there is a continuum between positive and negative social orientation.

Nowlis and Nowlis formulated the idea of the social orientation dimension of emotional behavior in studies dealing with the influence of drugs on moods. They found that the drug seconal had a social influence. The main hypothesis of the study was that people taking seconal would be more influenced by the mood of partners than were subjects who were given dramamine. The mood of companions as well as the nature of the task and the drug itself were found to influence the type of social orientation shown. When we are socially oriented we tend to share our feelings with others.

There can be no doubt that social and antisocial attitudes exist. Whether or not this attitudinal dimension should be regarded as major in the area of emotional arousal is open to question. Further research and study of the matter is needed.

The Relation between Moods and Emotions

Moods, as we noted in Chapter 1, are affects that are typically less intense, less disruptive, and of longer duration than emotions. A mood may last for hours, days, or weeks. There are moods of cheerfulness, depression, anxiety, resentment, amusement, excitement, and the like. A mood may flare up into an emotion. For example, a mood of resentment or hostility may build into an emotion of rage. John doesn't like the way the boss treats him. He feels he is forever being "put down." When the boss gives an important assignment to another worker one day, John suddenly blows up, his simmering resentment turning into pure rage. A mood of anxiety may build up into an emotion of fear or terror, depending upon circumstances. (Going to the doctor for another allergy test, Mary has a mood of apprehension. She remembers the painful needle pricks. When the doctor appears, she is frightened.) Or an emotion may taper off into a mood. Because of this relationship it is not always possible to draw a sharp line between emotions and moods. But, as we have said, moods tend to be chronic, persistent, affective states and emotional outbreaks are acute and disruptive.

Both moods and emotions are polarized and, like other affective arousals and states, moods vary between agreeable and disagreeable forms. Some moods, such as excitement, are relatively neutral in relation to pleasure, and have varying cognitive content and outward expression.

The conditions that determine or influence moods are complex. Nowlis (1953) investigated the effects of drugs upon moods and found that some drugs profoundly influence the affective state. He used a list of 100 to 200 adjectives and instructed subjects who had been given particular drugs to read it rapidly and check the words that characterized the mood they felt. For example, dramamine usually produced an increase in checking the words *tired, drowsy, detached, sluggish, disinterested, dull, lazy, retiring, withdrawn*; and a decrease in *businesslike, genial, industrious, talkative, cheerful, energetic.* Benzedrine gave an increase in the words *businesslike, talkative, capable, enterprising, independent,* and sometimes *nervous, jittery*; and a decrease in words like *lazy, languid, nonchalant.* The ratings of partners and other observers strongly confirmed the self-ratings.

It is common knowledge that the weather influences moods. On a crisp fall day most people feel invigorated. In the spring the mood "lightly turns to thoughts of love." On a hot summer day the mood is languid, relaxed. It has been found that the crime rate rises in times of humid weather in cities.

Transient moods are also influenced by events in the social environment such as grades, letters and money from home, the remarks of friends, dates, and similar conditions. (See Young, 1937.)

Variations in Mood

In a study of moods in relation to personality, Wessman and Ricks (1966) tested groups of Radcliffe and Harvard students and found that variations in mood, particularly in hedonic level, are common to all individuals. The well-known contrast between depression and elation is discussed in the following selection from their study:

> Depression, in general is characterized by a sense of sadness, dejection, and discouragement, accompanied by listlessness, apathy, and a lowering of self esteem, possibly with feelings of failure and worthlessness. . . . To varying degrees one withdraws from objects into oneself [and] feels apathetic and dull, alone and unwanted, yet with no particular desires or energy to participate with others. There is little satisfaction in personal relationships and work, yet energy is so lacking that there is no particular incentive or ability to improve the situation. . . . One may feel diffusely annoyed, irritable, anxious, or guilty. Often the sadness and fears seem vague and somehow incomprehensible, unattributable to particular circumstances or definite causes. . . . The depth and duration of these experiences vary; they may be mild and pass readily, or be profound and enduring.
>
> Elation, too, is an experience familiar to most people. There is a sense of gladness and joy. One feels encouraged, freshened, and renewed. Self-confidence soars. The world seems full and bright. The senses are lively, the mind keen and alert. Energy abounds. One is eager to communicate and participate with others. . . . Once again, there may be no apparent reason for this well-being. The exhilaration seems to be just there to be enjoyed and expressed as long as it lasts. (34)

Wessman and Ricks found two main variables in moods. First, there is the hedonic variable—the swing between elation and depression. Second, there is the variation in stability. Some persons have pronounced ups and downs in mood; others are relatively more stable. These two kinds of variation are independent of each other.

Happiness and Unhappiness

Wilson (1967) reviewed an extensive literature dealing with avowed happiness. In summarizing the alleged conditions that cause happiness, he described the happy individual as "a young, healthy, well-educated, well-paid, extroverted, optimistic, worry-free, religious, married person with high self-esteem, high job morale, modest aspirations, of either sex and a wide range of intelligence." The statement indicates some of the conditions associated with avowed happiness. Wilson does not tell us how many people are lucky enough to meet all these conditions of happiness! If we convert his summary into the negative form, we arrive at a picture of the unhappy individual as old, sickly, poorly educated, underpaid, introverted, pessimistic, anxious, irreligious, unmarried, and with a low level of self-esteem, low job morale, pretentious aspirations, of either sex, and a narrow range of intelligence! Most persons, fortunately, fall somewhere between these extremes.

Instead of relating happiness and unhappiness to physical, social, and mental conditions in this way, I would prefer to relate cheerful and depressed moods to a person's optimistic-pessimistic outlook on his own life. For most of us, happiness does not depend upon the abundance of things we possess. Happiness depends on our mental attitude, the way we look at things.

In actual life a person is never continuously happy or unhappy. An unhappy person can have rare moments of happiness, but they take a particular form as if he cannot trust them. A happy person can have periods of withdrawal and unhappiness, but these also take a particular form. Our moods return to their characteristic level. The deviation is not from complete apathy (absence of feeling) but from a prevailing normal mood or affective state which is physiologically determined and relatively constant.

In this chapter we have discussed many of the ways people have sought to understand human emotions and moods. We have learned that there are many dimensions of feelings—ways in which our affects vary and differ. In the next chapter we will examine the relation between feeling and knowing.

3 Feeling and Knowing

COEFFICIENT OF CORRELATION   A numerical index showing the degree of relationship between two variables. Coefficients varying between zero (no relation) and 1.00 indicate complete correspondence in a direct relation, while those varying from zero to -1.00 indicate a complete inverse relation.

HIERARCHICAL RANKING   Arrangement into a graded series of objects from high to low values or of persons from high to low power.

SEMANTIC DIFFERENTIAL   An instrument for studying statistically the degree of relationship between the meanings of words.

The English word *feeling* has several meanings. It refers to tactual perception: An object *feels* rough or smooth, sharp or dull, hot or cold, etc. It refers to organic states: We *feel* hungry or thirsty, drowsy or wakeful, sick or well, etc. It refers to affective arousals: We *feel* pleasantness or unpleasantness, anger, fear, excitement, etc. The word also has cognitive meanings: We *feel* the strength of an argument, the appropriateness of a remark, the nobility of an action, etc.

These various meanings all have reference to subjective conscious experience. *Feeling* is a mode of experiencing.

Traditional psychology has drawn a distinction between knowing and feeling. The cognitive processes include perception, memory, reasoning, creative imagination, fantasy, and the like. The affective processes and states include the whole gamut of *felt* experiences, including emotionalized attitudes, evaluative dispositions, and the like.

Both feeling and knowing are intimately related to action, to motivation. Every evangelist, propagandist, advertiser, and actor knows that words can produce feelings and action. Think of Patrick Henry's words: "Forbid it, Almighty God! I know not what course

others may take, but as for me, give me liberty, or give me death!"
The fiery orator aroused an emotional commitment to fight and resist
the English. Words and feelings do indeed move us.

INTROSPECTIVE STUDIES
OF PLEASANTNESS AND UNPLEASANTNESS

Where and *What* We Feel:
The Elementary Status
of Pleasantness and Unpleasantness

Throughout the history of experimental psychology, attempts have
been made to prove that the simple feelings of pleasantness and
unpleasantness are *sensory* elements of experience. Years ago, students
in the laboratory of E. B. Titchener tried to observe the affective
elements of pleasantness and unpleasantness *as such,* directly and apart
from the stimulating conditions that produced them. The experiment
turned out to be a frustrating chase for an elusive affective element.
The observers, however, reported that they *felt* pleasantness as a
bright, very diffuse pressurelike experience that seemed to be centered
in the chest. Unpleasantness was felt as a less diffuse and dull pressure
localized in the abdominal area. This seemed to indicate that if
pleasant and unpleasant feelings can be directly observed as *sensory*
processes, they probably do belong to the modality of touch rather
than to some other sensory area. (Consider the expression, "I was
touched by her friendliness.") Thus Titchener was able to conclude
that so far as affective processes can be observed, they are sensory. (For
other studies directly related to pleasantness and unpleasantness, see
also Nafe, 1924 and Henle, 1974.)

One difficulty with regarding pleasantness and unpleasantness as
sensory processes lies in the fact that there are no peripheral receptors
that invariably induce the affective qualities. These feelings can be
elicited in all sense departments—by odors, tastes, cutaneous and
intraorganic stimulations, colors and tones. Moreover, whether an
affective reaction is reported as pleasant or unpleasant varies with
internal bodily conditions such as satiation, deprivation, adaptation,
internal temperature, and the like. Are these processes sensory then?

Judgments and Values:
Pleasantness and Unpleasantness as Cognitions

Harvey A. Carr (1925), a psychologist of the Chicago functional
school, took it for granted that a perceived object and the organic

reactions that it evokes are the only observable contents that can be detected in the search for an affective element. Vague organic effects and reverberations, he said, are wrongly taken to be affective elements. Only as far as organic reverberations can be observed can they be considered sensory in nature.

For Carr, the term *affection,* within psychology, referred to the aspects of experience that cause us to label them as pleasant or unpleasant. An experience that is judged to be neither pleasant nor unpleasant is said to be lacking in affective tone, indifferent, hedonically neutral.

Carr believed that pleasantness and unpleasantness are judgments —meanings—based on normal reaction tendencies. Innately we are so organized that we normally react to certain stimulus situations so as to enhance, maintain, or repeat them. Other stimulus situations arouse negative adaptive behavior—responses that minimize or rid us of their stimuli which we do not repeat. For example, certain odors cause us to hold our breath or our nose, leave the vicinity, and avoid them in the future. Other odors cause us to take another whiff. A conscious experience is judged to be pleasant if it arouses the positive type of response and unpleasant if it arouses a negative reaction. Stimulus situations which arouse neither type of adaptive behavior are regarded as neutral. These judgments, based on normal reaction tendencies, are verbalized as pleasant or unpleasant. As an individual develops, however, primary judgments are modified by motivational and other influences.

The strength of Carr's judgmental theory of affection lies in the fact that innate positive and negative reactions to stimulations do assuredly occur. These reactions can be observed as behavioral processes. They are *felt* and *known* to exist.

You can see by now that *judging* things is going to lead us into a discussion of *evaluation*—forming values. Carr considered the nature of evaluation in relation to feeling. Pleasing things are regarded as good and valuable; they are desirable. Displeasing things are regarded as bad; they are undesirable and disapproved. A child identifies what is pleasant with good and what is unpleasant with bad. Later, however, he has to learn that some pleasant things are "bad"; and some unpleasant, "good." Obviously, a four-year-old child considers playing in the mud in a far different light than taking a bath! In the development of values, I believe, there are both affective (hedonic) and cognitive (judgmental) standards of evaluation.

Carr's judgmental theory of the affective processes raises an important question: Can the conscious experiences of pleasantness and unpleasantness be reduced to meaningful judgments? Or is there an experienced difference between *feeling* and *meaning*?

First Impressions:
Pleasantness and Unpleasantness
as Primary Evaluations

Arnold (1960, 1:74) defined feeling as *"a positive or negative reaction to some experience. Pleasure and pleasantness are positive reactions, varying only in intensity. They can be defined as a welcoming of something sensed that is appraised as beneficial and indicates enhanced functioning. Pain and unpleasantness are negative reactions of varying intensity and can be defined as resistance to something sensed that is appraised as harmful and indicates impaired functioning. What is pleasant is liked, what is unpleasant, disliked."* (Italics in original)

Central to Arnold's definition of feeling is the concept of appraisal, or evaluation, of sensed experience. She regards pleasantness and unpleasantness as simple evaluations which are not necessarily verbalized. There are built-in bodily structures that lead a naive organism to evaluate some sensory stimulations as positive and other stimulations as negative. Fragrant odors, sweet tastes, sexual stimulations, etc. are *felt* (evaluated) positively; the reaction therefore is positive. Foul odors, bitter tastes, painful stimulations, etc., are *felt* (evaluated) negatively; the reaction is negative.

Another kind of appraisal (that elicits emotion) is definitely cognitive and depends upon mental processes. Arnold argues that man and subhuman animals "intuitively" perceive certain environmental situations in certain lights—for example, as threatening, or as potential sources of food, etc. They react according to a *cognitive estimation* of the situation. In emotional behavior, as distinct from simple hedonic reactions, the immediate "intuitive" appraisal of the environmental situation is a factor of prime importance.*

Arnold's distinction between simple hedonic evaluations, on the one hand, and cognitive appraisals, on the other, is important. She recognizes that we are consciously aware of pleasant and unpleasant feelings; and she distinguishes between feelings and cognitive judgments. (Carr's judgmental theory implies a distinction between affection and cognition, but he is less explicit about the difference.)

---

* In the second volume of her scholarly treatise, Arnold considers the neural anatomy and physiology of the *estimative* (evaluative) systems. See also Chapter 4.

"Mixed Feelings": The Dynamic Incompatibility of Pleasantness and Unpleasantness

Can pleasantness and unpleasantness exist at the same time? More than fifty years ago, as a graduate student in Titchener's laboratory, I performed an experiment that dealt with so-called "mixed feelings"—alleged experiences in which pleasantness and unpleasantness coexist (Young 1918, 1930). More than 2000 attempts were made to please and displease observers simultaneously. For example, in a specific instance an observer might be offered a chocolate mint and while he was enjoying that, an annoying sound would be made. Each observer was instructed to report the temporal course of his affective experience, in terms of quality and intensity, during a 20-second period of time.

Two important generalizations were derived from this study: First, some of the observers distinguished between feeling and meaning. There was a difference between a *felt pleasantness* of definite intensity and temporal course (affection) and the *meaning of pleasantness*—e.g., a meaning that a stimulus situation was, is, or might become pleasant (cognition). Most of the evidence justified a distinction between *feeling* and *meaning,* even though some observers were not clear about the matter. Second, when the quality, intensity, and temporal course of feeling were unambiguously reported there were *no instances of coexisting pleasantness and unpleasantness.* These affective processes were found to be incompatible, dynamically opposed, antagonistic. Pleasantness and unpleasantness do not occur simultaneously.

FUNCTIONAL REPORTS OF FEELINGS AND ATTITUDES

Introspective observations require special training and may be influenced by laboratory atmosphere. However, there is a functional type of report that is relatively free from bias. Such a report is in the simple form, "I like it" or "I dislike it."

"I like it" is equivalent to the statement: "Let it continue, I want more." "I dislike it" is equivalent to the statement: "Let it terminate, stop, avoid it, don't repeat it." "I am indifferent to it" implies no positive or negative hedonic reaction.

These functional reports have been used in many studies of affective reactions to stimulations in all the senses. They have also been used in cognitive *attitude* studies that use no immediate affective arousals as, for example, in inventories of interests and aversions to occupations.

Hedonic Reactions to Odors

An example of the effectiveness of functional reports is found in an experiment on the hedonic reactions to odors done by Kniep, Morgan, and Young (1931). Chemically stable substances were presented under standard conditions. Each subject was instructed to smell a substance and immediately report whether he liked or disliked the odor.

Results of the experiment are shown in Figure 6. One hundred college students, ages 18 to 24, were tested. The percents of positive reports (liking) for these adults are arranged from high to low in the illustration. The tests were also made in two grammar schools of Champaign, Illinois, with 50 children, ages 7 to 9, and 50 children, ages 11 to 13.

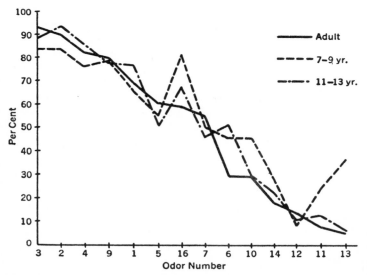

Figure 6. Rank order of odors for different age groups according to percentage reported as pleasant.* From Kniep, Morgan, and Young (1931).

* Chemical substances were selected to give a linear distribution of affective reactions from a high to a low percentage. The substances, indicated by number, were:
1. Camphor, 2. Methyl salicylate, 3. Vanillin, 4. p-Dichlorobenzene, 5. Menthol, 6. Phenol, 7. Acetophenone, 8. Nitrobenzene, 9. Geraniol, 10. Ethyl cinnamate, 11. n-Caproic acid, 12. Quinoline, 13. Heptyl aldehyde, 14. O-Bromotoluene, 15. di-Phenyl ether, 16. Empty bottle.

The rank order of percents of *liking* the odors is very similar for all age groups. Coefficients of correlation among the three age groups are exceedingly high—in the range of .91 to .96. This indicates that whatever determines the hedonic value of odors is relatively independent of age. Moreover, because most of the smells were unfamiliar to the subjects and because each odor was presented only once to a subject, we can assume that these hedonic values are independent of prior experiences—they are not learned.

Logic Versus Feelings: Cognitive and Hedonic Evaluations

Cognitive evaluations, as Arnold pointed out, are different from the simple hedonic evaluations of pleasant and unpleasant feelings. Cognitive evaluations may be purely logical and have no affective quality. Clear examples of cognitive evaluations are found in a study of *semantic differential* done by Osgood (1952) and Osgood and Suci (1955).

This impressive term, *semantic differential*, is simply the name of a method by which *meanings of words* can be analyzed. Pairs of words with opposite meaning (kind–cruel) can be represented as the extremes of a continuum:

kind_____:____:____:____:____:____:____cruel

Given such a continuum, other words can be placed somewhere between the extremes. Where, for example, would you place the word *pacifist?*

There are many such continua. The ratings of particular words have been found to be similar on different continua. For example, the ratings on the following pairs of words correlated .90 or better: fair–unfair, high–low, kind–cruel, valuable–worthless, Christian–anti-Christian, honest–dishonest. From this finding it follows that a few continua might be used for evaluating the meaning of many words.

By using a method of factor analysis, Osgood and Suci found that three main dimensions were sufficient to evaluate the meaning of most words. The first and major continuum is *evaluative.* It may be represented by verbal opposites such as good–bad, or beautiful–ugly. The second is *potency.* This may be represented by such combinations as strong–weak, or large–small. The third is *activity,* represented by words like active–passive, or fast–slow.

These three dimensions were found to converge into a single

composite of evaluation: good-strong-active *versus* bad-weak-passive.

Osgood said that *denotative* meanings are simply those that refer to specific objects, events, and relationships (ice cream, book, and other things to which the name refers). Connotative meanings are nonspecific and refer to an essential attribute of the thing denoted (pleasant, powerful, active). The semantic differential indicates connotative meanings only. It does not describe specific object meanings.

A question can be raised as to how the connotative meanings of words are related to feelings. Osgood and Suci found that *evaluation* was a major semantic variable. But is cognitive evaluation the same as feeling? I think not. You may have a terrible unpleasant headache (feeling) and at the same time agree with the judgment "This has been a pleasant day" (cognitive meaning).

The evaluative dimension has been found with different groups of subjects in different parts of the world. It is, therefore, reasonable to assume that there is an innate basis for connotative (cognitive) evaluations such as pleasant–unpleasant, good–bad, friend–enemy.

As distinct from cognitive judgments, let us assume that there are primary (nonspecific) biological "meanings" which are shown by acceptance or rejection, approach or withdrawal. These unverbalized "meanings," common to mankind and other animals, are *felt* subjectively and revealed objectively in behavior.

The philosopher Hume assumed that the mind of an infant is a blank slate upon which experience writes. But the human infant, like other organisms, is born with structures that provide innate biological meanings. Meanings and feelings are closely associated, fused, and both are related to action.

How We Know How We Feel:
The Two-way Relation between Feeling and Knowing

Affective arousals through sensory stimulations are current, ongoing events. They vary in sign (positive or negative), in intensity (strength), and in duration and temporal course.

Sensory stimulations have both cognitive and affective effects. Cognition, through sensory perception, presumably involves processes in the cerebral cortex. (See Appendix II for details regarding the bodily basis of feelings and emotions.) Information gained through perception is registered and the record (engram) is retained in the cerebral structures. In the next chapter we will see that affective arousals, through sensory stimulation, are mediated by processes in the limbic system of the brain. The affective awareness indicates to the conscious subject how he feels in a particular situation—how the stimulating situation affects him.

Affective arousals also yield cognitive information from inside the body. The subject *knows* (cognitively) that he is pleased or displeased, friendly or hostile, fearful, disgusted, and so on. The *memory* of how-I-feel-in-this-situation is recorded in the cerebrum along with other cognitive meanings. There is no evidence that the limbic-system mechanisms of affective arousal, as such, have memory. These neural mechanisms are illiterate; but *cognitive* awareness—knowledge of the emotion-inducing event—subsequently arouses an affective component. When you recall a past love affair, feelings are aroused.

Some memories of neutral events leave us cold. Others arouse joy, sorrow, hatred, fear, or some other emotion. There is thus a *cognitive* basis in memory for affective arousal.

Cognitive processes can direct and regulate the course of learning. If a child is told that his response is good or bad, right or wrong, correct or incorrect, this information directs the course of learning with or without any affective arousal. The cognitive information is *reinforcing* even though it brings no affective arousal. Learning through practice may be hedonically indifferent, and yet effective if it is well motivated. Some motivation is essential for learning to occur.

But it is also true that perception and memory can prompt strong emotional reactions. At a football game, for example, the spectators show signs of excitement when the teams run out on the field. If *your* team makes a touchdown, there is joyful excitement in your crowd. If *your* team loses the game, there may be a quieter mood.

Memories of past insults, of bereavements, of victories and defeats, of successes and failures, etc., can elicit real and intense feelings and emotions.

There is thus a two-way relation between affective and cognitive processes. The affective reaction yields information. This is an important factor in the organization of dispositions—habits, attitudes, interests, values, sentiments, etc. The cognitive processes—perceptions, memories, fantasies—are, in turn, potent sources of feeling and emotion.

And in conscious awareness, the cognitive and affective components fuse. We say we are "touched" by a kind and sympathetic remark. (Perhaps Titchener was right in placing *felt* pleasantness and unpleasantness in the modality of touch rather than some other sense modality.)

BEHAVIORAL STUDIES OF AFFECTIVE AROUSAL

A great deal of basic research upon emotional reactions has been done with chimpanzees, monkeys, cats, dogs, mice, rats, and other animals. This research helps us to understand, objectively and scientifically, the nature and importance of emotion in animal behavior. We should not forget that man himself, despite civilization, is an animal who has a place to fill and a role to play in nature.

I have made laboratory studies of the food preferences and appetites of rats. Some of this work is described in Appendix I. Brief reference to it is made here.

The Role of Learning:
Preference for Foods as Relative Evaluation

In testing rats for preference, using two kinds of foods, conditions can be arranged so that each food has the same opportunity of being accepted. Exposure of a pair of foods lasts for only a few seconds on each trial and the first food to elicit sustained acceptance is rated as the preferred food. (See Young, 1932, 1933.) The test foods in my 1930s studies were selected arbitrarily.* They differed widely in sensory quality. Despite this, there were marked consistencies in the individual and group choices. There were shown to be distinct hedonic levels in the choice of foods. This indicates that in both humans and animals, preferential behavior is learned. It starts, however, from innate affective reactions. During the early trials of a series there is often much indiscriminate behavior, but with repeated trials, experimental animals become increasingly consistent in their preferences. They clearly develop *habits of choice*. This fact demonstrates that *learning is an important factor in the growth of evaluative behavior*. A child has innate likes and dislikes. He *learns* to prefer some of the foods offered and may have to be trained to accept others. He has also to learn to

* For the foods used in this study and a chart showing an example of preferential hierarchies, see Appendix I.

accept values such as honesty, obedience, cleanliness, orderliness, and the like.

A test of preference reveals *relative* evaluation. If one food is consistently and significantly accepted rather than another, the implication is that the preferred food is *better* in some way than the nonpreferred. The preferred food is more palatable, more acceptable, than the nonpreferred. This is *relative* evaluation.

How Different Stimuli Are Perceived

In the study briefly described above, the test foods were very different in flavor and quality. Despite this, the foods were arranged into a hierarchy from low to high acceptability. We have found that foods with different appearance, texture, and taste may yet be equal or nearly equal in acceptability. They may occupy the same or nearly the same position in the hierarchical rank. Sensory quality and hedonic value are thus shown to be distinct properties of perception. (For a 1963 study by Young and Madsen demonstrating the hedonic equivalence of solutions of sodium-saccharin and sucrose, see Appendix I.)

The flavor of a food depends upon the integration of sensory qualities from different sense modalities—odor, taste, temperature, touch, appearance, and sound. The flavor is a unique combination. Flavors that differ widely in quality may still be acceptable. The foods in preferential hierarchies differ widely in sensory properties, yet different foods can be equally acceptable. (For a discussion and illustration of hedonic integration as it follows an algebraic principle of summation, see Appendix I.)

In an unpublished experiment, Clinton L. Trafton demonstrated hedonic integration across sense departments. He found that a food preference can be changed by giving rats a shock on the foot every time they touched the preferred solution. The foot shock had the same negative influence upon preference as the addition of quinine to a sucrose solution (see Appendix I).

Rodent and Human Evaluations

I have argued elsewhere that some rodent behavior is evaluative (Young, 1968). If a rat accepts a test food on the preference tester, that is a positive evaluation equivalent to the judgment *good, acceptable*. If the animal rejects a single food, that is a negative evaluation equivalent to the judgment *bad, unacceptable*. A preference test reveals relative evaluations. When a rat is offered a choice between two foods, a preferential discrimination develops. This development reveals a relative evaluation equivalent to the statement: Food A is *better than* food B.

It has been found that if pairs of test foods are systematically presented to rats for choice, the foods arrange themselves into a preferential hierarchy. The hierarchy is based upon relative palatability; it shows relative likes and dislikes for the flavors and textures of the different foods. Hedonic values, of course, should not be confused with nutritional values.

Human beings also develop value systems. If a situation arises in which an individual has to choose between two values, his choice reveals the relative importance, or potency, of the values. Have you ever seen a child automatically reach for the biggest piece of cake on the plate offered him—and then hesitate, grin sheepishly, and take a smaller piece? Here he has weighed his values and "thoughtfulness," taught him by his parents, has won out over a less "civilized" desire!

Values are shown in behavior. You value the things you spend time, effort, and money to attain. Positive values are desirable. A choice shows relative desirability. Negative values are attached to things you avoid or wish to avoid. Appetitive behavior, which we discussed briefly in Chapter 1, is positive; aversive behavior, negative.

Positive human values can be represented by words. They are objectives that are important to you. They are things you work for. Here is a typical list:

LOVE	HEALTH
KNOWLEDGE	AMBITION
SECURITY	RELIGION
FREEDOM	COMFORT
WEALTH	RECREATION

This list could be modified and extended. There are other basic values. How would you rank these values? What other values would you add? What would be your value hierarchy? Do your values sometimes collide? For instance, are you ever tempted to place comfort over recreation ("It's too *cold* to go skating!")? Or ambition over love?

Evaluative dispositions are based on experience. They change with time, place, and circumstance. They are relative to the environment in which you live. They are practically important.

GENERAL CONCLUSIONS

In this chapter we have considered the simple feelings of pleasantness and unpleasantness that depend upon stimulation of sense organs rather than the more complex emotions and moods considered in the previous chapter.

A basic question concerns the relation between *feeling* and *knowing*, between *affective arousal* and *cognition*. This question has been examined from three points of view: (1) the subjective point of view, which is concerned with the existential nature of pleasantness and unpleasantness as conscious experiences; (2) the naive functional view, which is implied in normal communications of everyday life; and (3) the objective, behavioral view.

From the subjective point of view a basic question was considered: whether the affective aspect of experience can be observed as sensation or whether positive and negative feelings are independent of sensory experience.

My conclusion is that pleasantness and unpleasantness, when elicited by sensory stimulations, acutely felt and referred to the perceived sensory objects, have an existential status that is separate from sensation. Pleasantness is *felt* (experienced) as a dynamic tendency to continue and repeat the sensory conditions that elicit it. Unpleasantness is *felt* as a dynamic tendency to terminate and avoid the sensory conditions.

Functional studies confirm the view that hedonic experiences differ in sign (positive or negative), intensity (strength), and duration (brief or lasting) and that they are integrated according to a law of algebraic summation that is different from the laws of sensory combination. (See Appendix I.)

There is a two-way relation between cognitive judgments or evaluations, on the one hand, and actual affective arousals, on the other. Introspective evidence and functional reports agree that pleasantness and unpleasantness are dynamically opposed and are antagonistic, positive and negative processes.

Finally, an objective, behavioral approach to the problems of affective arousal and cognition, with rats as subjects, has shown that these processes are distinct. Preference tests with different kinds of foods have shown that the level of acceptability is independent of sensory properties. Foods that differ widely in sensory properties may be equally acceptable and foods that are similar in sensory properties may differ in acceptability.

Affective arousals and cognitive expectations are distinct. In the next chapter we shall see that they depend upon separate neural mechanisms.

Receptor stimulations have two coordinate effects: (1) they yield sensory processes and cognitive information, and (2) they yield affective arousals and hedonic information about how stimulations *affect* you, the experiencing subject. The hedonic and the sensory information are combined in such a way that the object is evaluated as good or bad, pleasant or unpleasant, acceptable or unacceptable. A similar bipolarity of evaluation appears in the purely cognitive appraisal or estimation of complex environmental situations.

Finally, affective processes organize dispositions and value hierarchies in both animal and man. These evaluative dispositions are of great practical importance. They can be studied objectively. Therefore, there is an objective, as well as a subjective basis for a possible science of values.

4 Physiological Theories of Feeling and Emotion

TERMS YOU WILL MEET IN THIS CHAPTER

HOMEOSTASIS The internal physiochemical states of relative stability and constancy; a balanced, steady state.

NERVOUS SYSTEM All the nerve cells in an organism: includes those in the brain, spinal cord, ganglia, nerves, and nerve centers. The nervous system organizes and controls responses to stimuli. Its lowest level is the *spinal cord* and *medulla;* it is here that spinal reflexes are integrated. The second level contains *thalamus, hypothalamus,* and other structures in the *limbic system.* These are structures related to the arousal of affective reactions. The highest level is the *cerebral cortex,* which is essential for cognition, including perception, memory, etc.

AUTONOMIC NERVOUS SYSTEM This consists of the *sympathetic* and *parasympathetic* divisions of the nervous system which control the motor functions of the vital organs—heart, lungs, etc.—as well as the smooth muscles, and the blood and lymph vessels. The nervous system as a whole contains *afferent neurons,* which conduct impulses from sensory receptors to the central nervous system, and *efferent neurons,* which carry impulses away from the central nervous system to the effector cells of muscles and glands. (See Appendix II.)

VISCERAL Refers to heart, lungs, stomach, spleen, liver, etc.—the soft organs located in the body cavity. Visceral changes are regulated by the autonomic nervous system.

As we have seen, early investigators of the emotions related the passions to bodily changes in the heart, lungs, muscles, sex organs, brain, blood, nerves, and other parts of the body. Even today we hear such expressions as "Her heart isn't in it," "What gall he has," "I can't stomach that," "That takes plenty of guts." Speculations about feelings and emotions are as old as human thought. (See Gardiner,

Metcalf, and Beebe-Center, 1937.) But modern attempts to define and distinguish feelings and emotions *solely* in terms of bodily changes have failed. Today it is generally recognized that to understand conscious feelings and emotions it is necessary to take account of the inducing situations and the mental history of a person as well as the physiological processes.

The human nervous system is very complex, and a full discussion of it would involve us in a lot of technical details. In Appendix II the more important anatomical parts are described. For present purposes it will be sufficient to understand that the organization of behavior and experience occurs at three levels of integration.

Levels of Neural Integration and Control

It is convenient to think of the nervous system as organized at three levels. The lowest level is that of the spinal cord and medulla. At this level the spinal reflexes are integrated. As we will see later in this chapter, Sherrington has shown a reciprocal relation between the processes of excitation and inhibition.

The second, or intermediate level contains structures above the medulla and below the cerebral cortex. At this level are structures known to be related to the arousal of affective reactions: the thalamus and hypothalamus, the limbic system, the amygdala, and closely related structures of the old brain. (See Appendix II.) Patterns of response that appear during emotions are integrated at this level, such as the rage pattern including growling, hissing, protrusion of the claws in cats, startle and fear in humans, and other emotional patterns. The vital processes that are essential to survival are also regulated through the autonomic nervous system at this intermediate level. These processes include sleep and wakefulness, the regulation of feeding and drinking, the processes of sexual and maternal behavior, and instinctive patterns of defense and aggression.

There is also chemical regulation at this intermediate level. Hormones that circulate in the blood have specific effects upon neural centers. The pituitary body, that master gland, interacts reciprocally with the gonads and has a profound influence upon feelings and emotions. (See Appendix II.)

The third and highest level of neural integration is the cerebral cortex. At this level there is processing of information gained through environmental and bodily sensory stimulations. There is storage and retrieval of information in memory. This neocortex (new brain), as distinct from the paleocortex (old brain), is essential for cognition, including perception and attention, memory, planning for future behavior, and other regulatory processes.

The cerebral cortex is involved in problems, conflicts, frustrations, excitements, the building and release of tension. These are the conditions that elicit emotions. Emotional disorganization and the organization of intentional behavior involves the organism as a whole. The relation between cerebral processes and arousals at the level of the midbrain and old brain is of prime importance in understanding emotions and feelings.

The physiologist is concerned with what goes on inside the body when feelings and emotions are experienced. He wants to know how physiological (neural) events (electrical and chemical) are related to subjective and objective psychological phenomena.

A tremendous amount of research has been done in the broad field of physiological psychology. We will consider only a small portion of this work insofar as it relates to feelings and emotions. Some of the terms we will meet—such as *autonomic nervous system, homeòstasis, hypothalamus*—may puzzle you, but don't let that scare you. All the studies we will look at have been undertaken to better understand our emotions. Learning about such investigations will help us to view our feelings—our affective processes—in a new light with deeper insight.

MAINTAINING STABILITY: HOMEOSTASIS AND EMOTION

Now that we understand a bit more about the way our bodies are constructed in relation to receiving and interpreting stimuli, we can look at the important concept of homeostasis to see how this relates to the affective processes and especially to physiological theories of the emotions.

Claude Bernard, the great French physiologist, distinguished between the internal environment *(milieu intérieur)*, consisting mainly of the fluids within which the cells of the body live, and the external environment *(milieu extérieur)*, which surrounds the organism as a whole. The internal environment varies, physically and chemically, within narrow limits. Variations outside these limits endanger the existence of the cells and hence of life itself.

The Harvard physiologist, Walter B. Cannon (1932), coined the word *homeostasis* to designate internal physicochemical states of relative stability and constancy. He explained that the word does not imply something set and immobile, a stagnation—rather, homeostasis is a condition that varies but that remains relatively constant. The coordinated physiological processes which maintain most of the steady states in the organism are complex and peculiar to living beings—they involve the brain, nerves, heart, lungs, kidneys and spleen, all working cooperatively.

To help understand physiological homeostasis, here are some examples:

1. The internal temperature of the body remains relatively constant despite wide variations in external temperatures. A man can survive in arctic regions at 30°F or more below zero. You can go to the desert, where temperatures are above 120°F, without an appreciable increase in your body temperature. Internal temperature does vary with disease and health but, as we know, it varies within a narrow range. A rise of temperature above normal is considered a symptom of disorder.

2. The water content of the blood and lymph must be maintained at a relatively fixed level as a condition of survival. Failure of an organism to obtain and ingest water results in dehydration of the tissues and increased concentration of mineral salts within the blood and lymph. When there is a deficit of water in the body fluids, thirst normally leads to the intake of water with removal of the deficit.

3. The oxygen content of the blood is maintained at a relatively constant level through the elaborate mechanisms of respiration. Red blood corpuscles carry oxygen from the lungs to tissues throughout the body. In times of stress their concentration is increased through mechanical action of the spleen; this facilitates the process of oxygenation. In drowning, the oxygen supply is cut off at the source; carbon dioxide accumulates in the blood with a fatal result.

4. The acidity of the blood is held remarkably constant at a point near neutrality. A slight shift toward acidity results in coma and death. A shift toward alkalinity produces convulsions. The maintaining of a relatively constant pH in the blood is one of the conditions of life.

Similarly, there are homeostases of blood sugar, blood sodium, blood calcium, and other minerals, of blood fat, protein, and other dietary elements.

During emotional upsets the normal physiological processes that control homeostasis are disturbed. If you are frightened by a snarling dog, your heart beats rapidly, the process of digestion is slowed down or stopped, and blood is directed away from the stomach to the muscles and brain where it is needed for action. When the crisis is over, there is a gradual return to normal homeostatic regulation.

Curt Richter (1942) extended the homeostatic principle by showing how behavior helps an organism maintain a physicochemical steady state. If homeostasis is disturbed, behavior compensates for the disturbance and tends to restore the steady state. This principle has been shown clearly in many experiments with both animals and human beings.

Self-regulatory behavior appears, for example, in the selection of foods. When the adrenal glands of rats are surgically removed, the animals normally die in 10 to 15 days as a result of loss of sodium chloride through the urine. In one experiment, Richter (1936) found that when the operated rats were given free access to a 3 percent sodium chloride solution they ingested several times the normal amount of the salty fluid, keeping themselves alive indefinitely, in seemingly good health. Some rats increased their salt intake tenfold. The increased appetite for salt, Richter argued, served to maintain homeostasis and life itself.

Richter concluded that "in human beings and animals the effort to maintain a constant internal environment or homeostasis constitutes one of the most universal and powerful of all behavior urges or drives."

Homeostasis and Pleasure–Unpleasure

In an important series of recent experiments, Cabanac (1971) has shown that a stimulus can be felt as pleasant or unpleasant depending upon its *usefulness* in maintaining homeostasis. He performed experiments that involved temperatures, tastes, and odors.

In the temperature experiments, people's hands were immersed in water; they were directed to report on their feelings of pleasantness or unpleasantness when the left hand was stimulated for 30 seconds by water of known temperature. The responses differed according to the thermal state of each person. The temperatures of the bath (15° and 45°C) were between the lower and upper thresholds of pain—thus pain was not a factor involved in the responses. A person who was chilly felt pleasant when the hand was immersed in hot water; one who was uncomfortably warm experienced pleasant feelings when the hand was immersed in very cold water. Cabanac argues that pleasure is felt in the presence of a stimulus which helps to maintain a relatively constant internal temperature, which for man is 37°C (98.6°F).

The affective-motivational component of perception, Cabanac concluded, depends upon signals from inside the body, since in his experiments exactly the same physical stimulus was perceived as either pleasant or unpleasant depending upon a departure from the constant normal body temperature.

In studies with tastes and odors, Cabanac found that a sweet-tasting sucrose and an orange odor were pleasant when the subject had fasted, but that these were perceived as unpleasant after the subjects had swallowed 100 grams of glucose in water. The internal signals during satiation, therefore, regulate the hedonic effects. The nature of these internal signals is not known.

Cabanac's findings are theoretically important because they demonstrate that positive and negative feelings depend upon and regulate internal bodily processes as well as the behavior of the organism in relation to environment.

In general, feelings depend upon our internal bodily state. Feelings of hunger and thirst obviously depend upon a lack of the food and water required to maintain homeostasis. Feelings of fatigue depend upon overexertion. Feelings of drowsiness occur when we need sleep. Cabanac's experiment shows why a swim is pleasant on a hot day and a warm bath is pleasant on a cold day. Our feelings, therefore, help to maintain an internal steady state, or homeostasis. We speak of *feelings*, not emotions, because emotions are reactions to perceived or known environmental situations. Emotions arise in our attempt to cope with environmental problems and situations.

PHYSIOLOGICAL THEORIES OF EMOTION

Although speculations about the emotions are ancient, discussion of modern theories usually begins with the James-Lange theory. Darwin, it is true, was greatly concerned with the outward manifestations of emotions, but he paid little attention to the subjective, conscious aspect. His contemporaries, however, regarded emotion as a *conscious* event that is outwardly expressed.

The James-Lange Theory of Emotion:
Emotion as a Conscious Experience

William James (1913) believed that emotion was a *conscious* experience characterized by organic sensation and expressed outwardly in behavior. He was much impressed by the physiological changes that appear when an individual is emotionally aroused.

James quoted C. Lange, a Danish physiologist, to show that in grief, for example, there may be paralysis of voluntary movement, movement that is slow and heavy and without strength, a weak voice, bent neck with head hanging or "bowed down," eyes large in appearance, bloodlessness of the skin, dry mouth, and in nursing women a diminishing of milk. James quoted Darwin to present some of the organic symptoms of fear: wide-open eyes and mouth, motionless posture and breathlessness, violently beating heart, paleness of skin, cold sweat, erect hairs, trembling of the muscles, dry mouth, arms protruded as if to avert some danger, and so on. James quoted Mantegazza in listing such bodily changes in emotion as withdrawal of the trunk, contraction or closure of the eyes, frowning, display of the teeth and contracting jaws, deep inhaling, automatic repetition of one word or syllable, redness or pallor of the face, dilation of the nostrils, standing up of the hair on the head, and so on.

James was pessimistic about bringing law and order out of this mass of descriptive details in the literature of emotion. He said that if we go through the whole list of emotions and examine their bodily manifestations, we only "ring the changes on the elements" which these emotions involve. Nevertheless, he went on to state his theory in a paragraph which, perhaps, has been more widely quoted than any other writing in the literature of emotion:

> Our natural way of thinking about these coarser emotions is that the mental perception of some fact excites the mental affection called the emotion, and that this latter state of mind gives rise to the bodily expression. My theory, on the contrary, is that *the bodily changes follow directly the perception of the exciting fact, and that our feeling of the same changes as they occur IS the emotion.* Common-sense says, we lose our fortune, are sorry and weep; we meet a bear, are frightened and run; we are insulted by a rival, are angry and strike. The hypothesis here to be defended says that this order of sequence is incorrect, that the one mental state is not immediately induced by the other, that the bodily manifestations must first be interposed between, and that the more rational statement is that we feel sorry because we cry, angry because we strike, afraid because we tremble, and not that we cry, strike, or tremble, because we are sorry, angry, or fearful, as the case may be. Without the bodily states following on the perception, the latter would be purely cognitive in form, pale, colorless, destitute of emotional warmth. We might then see the bear, and judge it best to run, receive the insult and deem it right to strike, but we should not actually *feel* afraid or angry.

For James the essential point was that *an emotion is an awareness of bodily changes as they occur.* When there is a situation that arouses bodily changes reflexively, the awareness of these intraorganic changes constitutes the emotion.

James, in arguing for his theory, pointed out, first, that no one doubts that psychological objects and situations do arouse bodily changes through prearranged physiological mechanisms and that in emotion these changes extend through the entire organism. Second, every one of these bodily changes is *felt*, acutely or obscurely, the moment it occurs. Third, if we fancy some strong emotion, and try to abstract from it the consciousness of its bodily symptoms, there is nothing left behind. "What kind of an emotion of fear would be left if the feeling neither of quickened heart-beats nor of shallow breathing, neither of trembling lips nor of weakened limbs, neither of goose-flesh nor of visceral stirrings, were present, it is quite impossible for me to think. Can one fancy the state of rage and picture no ebullition in the chest, no flushing of the face, no dilatation of the nostrils, no clenching of the teeth, no impulse to vigorous action, but in their stead limp muscles, calm breathing, and a placid face? The present writer, for one, certainly cannot. . . ."

The essential features of the James-Lange theory of emotion are these: First, emotion is assumed to be a *conscious* sensory experience. Second, there is a sequence of: (a) perception of an exciting fact, and (b) perception of involuntary bodily changes. Third, the theory implies causal relations. Do we run *because* we feel afraid? Or do we feel afraid *because* we tremble, have an impulse to run, etc.? Taken literally, these questions imply a mind-body interaction; and they raise a profound philosophical problem: that of the relation between subjective and objective events, between mind and body.

The Pattern-Reaction Theory:
Emotion as a Behavior Pattern

C. G. Lange, in 1885, published a paper in which he emphasized that vasomotor disturbances are real outcomes of affective experiences. The vasomotor changes have secondary manifestations; but Lange regarded emotion as a *visceral* pattern of reaction that is regulated through the autonomic nervous system. (See Table 1-A in Appendix II, page 161.)

Watson (1919), an early behaviorist, stated in his major definition that *"an emotion is an hereditary pattern-reaction involving profound changes of the bodily mechanism as a whole, but particularly of the visceral and glandular systems."* Bard (1934), emphasized that "in his experimental work the physiologist (as distinguished from the student of subjective experience) considers emotions as behavior patterns." Much later Ax (1953), using human subjects, claimed that fear and anger can be differentiated in terms of the *pattern of physiological changes*.

Wenger (1950) does not speak of emotion as *inducing* bodily changes nor of bodily changes as *inducing* conscious emotion. Rather, he regards a visceral response as *itself* an emotion. For example, three or four visceral patterns can be detected in sexual excitement. Wenger would accept these observed patterns *as* emotions, speaking of emotions per se only insofar as patterns can be distinguished from the continuous state of homeostasis.

Many patterns of reaction have been observed and studied. As a single example, consider the pattern of rage that appears during hostile attack. In most animals, patterns of reaction appear which are unambiguous in their biological meaning. The entire organism becomes integrated for a fight—for a vigorous, hostile attack upon an enemy. Nature has produced, through countless centuries of evolution, the claws and teeth of the tiger, the fangs of the snake, the sting and poison sac of the insect, etc., as instruments of offense and defense. The internal neurohumoral and muscular systems are organized naturally for a serious life-and-death struggle, and in the human body there is a similar organization. Hostile behavior is primitive; it depends upon deeply ingrained bodily organization.

It has been demonstrated that the rage pattern appears in dogs and cats even after surgical removal of the cerebral cortex. In the decorticate cat, for example, there is a remarkable exhibit of rage which includes lashing of the tail, arching of the trunk, protrusion of the claws and clawing movements, snarling or growling, hissing, turning of the head from side to side with attempts to bite, rapid panting with mouth open, movements of the tongue to and fro. Along with this there is erection of the hair on the tail and back, sweating of the toe pads, dilation of the pupils, increase in heart rate and arterial pressure, retraction of the nictitating membrane (a transparent eyelid), and (as physiologically determined) an abundant secretion of adrenalin and increased level of blood sugar—which level may rise to five times its normal level. These manifestations appear in "fits" which last from a few seconds to many minutes with intervening periods of quiet during which a "fit" can be evoked by the slightest disturbance of the animal, such as pinching the tail or the loose skin of the flank.

With decorticate dogs the rage pattern is quite similar. There are such manifestations as baring of the teeth, vicious biting and snapping, snarling or growling, struggling. These symptoms are readily prompted by stimulation, e.g., forcibly restraining the animal or rubbing his skin. See Figure 7.

Removal of the cerebral cortex makes the rage patterns of both dogs and cats more easily elicited than in normal animals. The rage pattern in decorticate animals has been described as "sham rage" on the

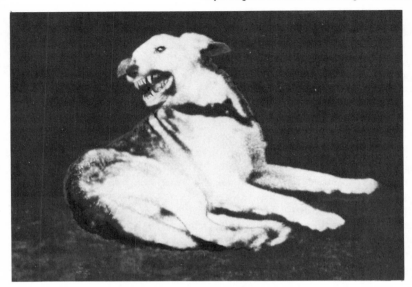

Figure 7. The pattern of "sham rage" in the decorticate dog. From a film by Dr. E. A. Culler depicting the behavior of a decorticate dog.

assumption that these animals cannot *feel* any emotion. This assumes, however, that consciousness is limited to cortical function. We know that the subcortical centers of affective arousal are illiterate and lack memory. There is no way of knowing about the conscious states of animals that have had the cerebral cortex removed. But the outward expressions of rage in decorticate animals are very similar to those associated with intense conscious emotions.

A human being can remember that yesterday he was angered, frightened, sexually aroused, or whatever. But this is because the brain is intact. Humans have subcortical neural structures (thalamus, hypothalamus, etc.) that are similar to those in other animals and known to control patterns of emotional behavior. Our memory of previous emotions, however, depends upon impressions (engrams) that are left in the cerebral cortex. Our memory re-arouses previous feelings and emotions. (See Appendix II.)

Various other patterns of reaction that occur during emotion have been described, including the startle patterns, fear, sexual response, disgust, crying and weeping, smiling and laughing, and a variety of patterns of escape and defense. (See Young, 1961.)

The view that emotion is a pattern of reaction appeals strongly to physiologists and physiological psychologists. There are a number of reasons for this: (1) Patterns of response are prominent parts of emotional behavior. (2) Temporospatial patterns can be observed objectively and the conditions of their occurrence controlled. (3) Like the simpler reflexes, emotional patterns can be conditioned and the conditioned emotional responses extinguished. (4) Patterns can be described in terms of stimulus and response. The pattern-reaction concept fits smoothly into the S-R model. (5) The neural mechanisms that integrate some of these emotional patterns have been located in subcortical regions of the nervous system and some of them have been accurately described.

However, I do not believe that it is enough to define an emotion simply as a patterned reaction. Patterns have been described as "fragments" of emotions—as reactions that occur during emotional disturbances. The emotional patterns are complex, being made up of many reflexive elements. A sharp distinction between simple reflexes and complex emotional patterns is arbitrary and has never been drawn. Simple reflexes and emotional patterns are innate, instinctive.

Finally, the pattern-reaction concept disregards the disorganization and loss of cerebral control that occurs in emotional upsets. When you are terribly frightened you sometimes lose all control of yourself. The pattern-reaction concept also disregards the subjective or conscious aspects of affective arousals. Thus the pattern-reaction definition of emotion, though sound, can be considered only a partial view of a complex event.

Cannon's Emergency Theory: Emotion as Readiness to Act

Basic emotional behavior arises in situations that threaten your life. You carry out daily activities scarcely aware of the primary need for oxygen. But suppose you are suddenly plunged into water and are in danger of drowning. Immediately there is a frantic struggle to reach the air. The emotion is one of fear or terror with a high level of arousal. Behavior and consciousness are dominated by the critical situation.

Walter B. Cannon (1929), Professor of Physiology in the Harvard Medical School, made extensive studies of the bodily changes that occur during pain, hunger, fear, rage, and great emotional excitement. His subjects were cats made emotional by the barking of a dog.

Cannon demonstrated that during a biological crisis when an animal must fight or run for its life and when bloodshed is likely, profound and widespread bodily changes occur which mobilize the energy resources of the body for a vigorous and prolonged struggle. The emergency reaction produces bodily changes by a diffuse discharge across the sympathetic nervous system, supported in part by the secretion of the adrenal glands. (See Appendix II.) In summarizing his many experiments he stated the emergency theory of emotion in these words:

> Every one of the visceral changes that have been noted—the cessation of processes in the alimentary canal (thus freeing the energy supply for other parts); the shifting of blood from the abdominal organs to the organs immediately essential to muscular exertion; the increased vigor of contraction of the heart; the discharge of extra blood corpuscles from the spleen; the deeper respiration; the dilation of the bronchioles; the quick abolition of the effects of muscular fatigue; the mobilizing of sugar in the circulation—these changes are *directly serviceable in making the organism more effective in violent display of energy which fear or rage or pain may involve.* (225–26)

Cannon's emergency theory of emotion was formulated during World War I when the distinction between war and peace was obvious to all. The discharge across the sympathetic network, Cannon argued, puts the organism on a wartime basis. This discharge during stress mobilizes the energy reserves of the body and prepares it for facing an emergency. In times of peace, Cannon argued, the parasympathetic nerves control conservative and upbuilding functions of anabolism. The peacetime functions of the parasympathetic nerves are antagonistic to and incompatible with the sympathetico-adrenal discharge and thus do not occur simultaneously with the emergency reaction.

Cannon's theory is obviously not a complete theory of emotion. It does not deal with excited pleasant emotions of joy, laughter, ecstasy; nor with depressed emotions of sorrow, weeping, grief; nor with such human emotions as jealousy, embarrassment, shame, remorse. In these and other emotions there are patterns of visceral changes controlled by the simultaneous action of the sympathetic and parasympathetic systems. Emotional reactions involve the autonomic nervous system as a whole and not merely the sympathetic network.

Moreover, an emotional crisis is an occasional event. The auto-nomic nervous system is on duty twenty-four hours a day regulating vital bodily processes.*

The Activation Theory: Levels of Arousal

In discussing Lindsley's (1951) concept of activation (page 23), I described a continuum showing different levels of arousal. Emotion was represented as a highly excited state of the organism. The neural center of emotional arousal lies in the reticular activating system of the brain stem, diagrammed in Figure 8. (See also Figure A-7 in Appendix II, p. 162.)

The activating system has two functional parts: (1) A network of neurons located at the levels of the medulla, midbrain, hypothalamus,

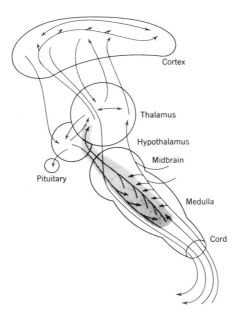

Figure 8. A schematic representation to show location of neural structures and probable pathways in the reticular activating system. After Lindsley (1951).

* For further details and discussion see Young (1973b, 244–55).

and subthalamus, and (2) a system of fibers that project diffusely from nuclei in the thalamus to the cerebral cortex. Arrows indicate the direction of conduction of neural impulses into the brain stem reticular formation and upward, through diffuse pathways to the cerebral cortex. Other arrows indicate that there is a downward conduction from the cortex to the reticular activating formation.

There are in fact two kinds of neural pathways from receptors to the brain. In the classical conception of sensory function, the afferent input from receptors was via the great projection system only: from sensory nerves to sensory tracts, thence to sensory nuclei in the thalamus, and on to the projection areas of the cortex. There is a second kind of excitation, however. Through collateral fibers, the reticular network is activated. The excitations trickle through a tangled thicket of fibers and synapses; there is a mixing up of messages so that specific information is completely lost and excitations are distributed to wide areas of the cortex. This diffuse excitation serves to tone up the cortex with a background of supporting action which is necessary for the specific messages to have their effect. The cortical excitation itself feeds back into the activating system to increase arousal.

Hebb (1955) has pointed out that research on activation has shown a physiological basis for the *energetic* view of drive. He points to two functions: (1) A *cue function* related to guiding and steering behavior through receptor stimulations; and (2) an *arousal* or *vigilance function* which is essential to cue function and motivation.

Hebb pointed out that some organisms actually *seek* excitement that has no relation to the primary drives. People welcome the risk of a roller coaster or mountain climbing or a problem to be solved. Such facts make sense when we think of the arousal function in terms of diffuse cortical excitation rather than in terms of specific primary drives.

One weakness of a one-dimensional theory of activation is that it does not account for positive and negative hedonic effects. Other research, considered below, removes that limitation.

Hedonically neutral activation has to do with survival activities; it supports cautious and alert observation, exploratory and manipulative behavior, and other useful reactions. Through observations and explorations an organism becomes acquainted with its surroundings. Dangers and threats to security, as well as potential food and companions, are perceived. Much perception of the environment is positive but hedonically neutral.

The Neural Basis of Pleasure and Unpleasure

In 1953, James Olds was experimenting with electrodes implanted in the brains of healthy, normal rats, attempting to stimulate the reticular activating formation to discover whether this would increase alertness and facilitate the process of learning.

Quite by accident, an electrode was implanted in a part of the brain called the anterior commisure. When the rat's brain was stimulated at this point the animal acted *as if* he liked it. If the rat's brain was electrically stimulated when he came to a specific point in an open field, he would, sooner or later, return to that spot and sniff. Repeated stimulations of that part of the brain caused the animal to spend more and more time at the place where the brain stimulations were received. Olds discovered that the rat could be trained to go to any spot in a maze if the "pleasure center" was consistently stimulated when he arrived at that spot. For example, in a T-maze the animal could be trained to turn consistently to the left or to the right if he was rewarded solely by electrical brain stimulations. A hungry rat with food at both ends of the T-maze would stop at any point where he was rewarded by electrical brain stimulations. (See Olds and Milner, 1954.)

At about the same time Delgado, Roberts, and Miller (1954) were experimenting with electrodes implanted in the brains of cats. In one experiment five cats were trained before the operation to turn a wheel in order to stop an electric shock delivered through a grid on the floor. A buzzer anticipated the shock by 5 seconds; if the cats learned to rotate the wheel while the buzzer sounded, they could avoid the frightening sound and the painful shock. Training continued until the animals had learned to respond to the buzzer and thus avoid the shock.

After this training, electrodes were implanted and the cats allowed to recover from the operation. After recovery, they were healthy and normally active. Then they were tested with electrical brain stimulations. Some animals turned the wheel immediately at the first stimulation. Others appeared to be confused by the motor side effects of the simulations, but learned in very few trials to turn the wheel and avoid the shock. The habit of turning the wheel thus transferred readily from external to internal "punishment."

Following these pioneer experiments, the research upon intracranial stimulation has mushroomed until today there is an immense literature upon brain centers for "reward" and "punishment."

Routtenberg (1968) postulated *two* arousal systems rather than a single activating system. Arousal System I includes the reticular activating system of the brain stem; this system maintains arousal of the organism and provides drive for the activation of organized responses. Arousal System II includes the limbic and related neural systems; it provides control of responses elicited through incentive-related stimuli (food, sex, temperature, pain, etc.). System II is a diffuse, nonspecific, inhibitory system. The two arousal systems are reciprocally related. The anatomical and physiological details, however, are far from clear.

In general, there are apparently two diffuse, nonspecific, activating systems. One is positive, excitatory; the other is negative, inhibitory. The two systems are reciprocally related. A reciprocal relation must be assumed to exist in order to account for the facts of hedonic integration.

There are, indeed, neural mechanisms that regulate pleasurable and unpleasurable affective arousals. Heath (1964) reported some results with human patients who voluntarily agreed to have electrodes permanently implanted in the septal area of the limbic system. (See Appendix II, page 162.) With stimulation in this area, patients reported pleasant, good, happy feelings, pleasant memories, and some reported sexual feelings. With electrodes implanted at other locations, self-stimulations produced distress and unhappy thoughts, but distress could be relieved and comfort restored by pressing the septal button.

These observations are theoretically important because they demonstrate a direct relation between subjective feelings of pleasantness and unpleasantness and internal self-stimulations.

The Role of the Cerebral Cortex in Emotion

What part does the cerebral cortex play in our emotions? A prominent feature of emotional reactions, as James and others pointed out, is the presence of widespread visceral changes throughout the body—the blush of shame, the pallor of fear, the rise in blood pressure in sexual excitement and anger, the increase of heart rate, etc. These changes, as we have seen, are controlled by the autonomic nervous system. (See Appendix II.)

There are also specific patterns of reaction in the skeletal musculature that are regulated by the central nervous system—the baring of the teeth, the growl, hiss, arching of the back, clawing movements, and in man smiling, laughing, crying, and so on.

How are these changes related to functions of the brain? There have been several answers.

Cannon (1927, 1931), in a critique of the James-Lange theory, argued that even cats and dogs with the cerebral cortex removed show normal patterns of rage, fear, disgust, and other emotions. This means that these emotional patterns cannot be organized in the cerebral cortex. Cannon theorized that the cortex provides a constant inhibitory action on the emotional centers of the thalamus. An emotion-inducing situation produces *cortical disinhibition*, which makes a specific response possible. A person's perception of a threatening situation, then, would free the cortex from its normal inhibition and thus release the emotional patterns. Incoming sensory impulses from viscera and skeletal musculature are what constitute the essence of emotional experience.

Decorticate animals are not as well coordinated and precise in fighting as are intact animals, however. The intact animal responds with rage upon the approach of a familiar enemy and organizes his responses to the danger more effectively.

Another view of the relation between the cerebral cortex and emotion is that of Arnold.

Arnold (1960, I: 182) defines emotion as *"the felt tendency toward anything intuitively appraised as good (beneficial), or away from anything intuitively appraised as bad (harmful). This attraction or aversion is accompanied by a pattern of physiological changes organized toward approach or withdrawal. The patterns differ for different emotions."* (italics in original)

The essential feature of this definition, as we saw in Chapter 3, is an emphasis on appraisal, evaluation of the situation that induces emotion. In other words, something must be known, through perception and memory or in imagination, before it can be feared, hated, desired. It is the understanding (cognitive estimation) of a situation that determines the kind of emotion that will be aroused. For example, an encounter with a grizzly bear in the mountains elicits fear but the perception of a similar bear in the zoo is just an interesting, nonemotional experience.

Arnold agrees with James that the emotional response involves involuntary changes in viscera and skeletal muscles. The feedback from these peripheral changes, Arnold states, is appraised in terms of how-I-feel-in-this-situation. According to James-Lange theory, this feedback *constitutes* the conscious emotion.

Arnold's appraisal-excitatory theory of emotion emphasizes the *cognitive function of the cerebral cortex in eliciting emotion.* The cognitive appraisal of events and situations precedes and is the immediate cause of emotions. This immediate, "intuitive," estimation *excites* emotional responses.

Grossman (1967) has criticized the theories of Cannon and Arnold, saying that the cerebral cortex exercises a *dual* control over the lower neural centers. Cannon emphasized the *inhibitory* (negative) influence and Arnold the *excitatory* (positive) influence. *Both* are known to exist. Moreover, some cortical areas are excitatory with respect to specific emotional targets and inhibitory with respect to other targets.

All things considered, it appears that the neurophysiology of emotion is still rather speculative and not too well understood. (For further details see Young, 1973a and 1973b.)

Acceptance or Rejection Reactions: Integration and Disintegration at the Cerebral Level

Years ago Sherrington (1911) demonstrated the integrative action of the nervous system at the level of the spinal cord. In his classic experiments with reflexes in dogs he proved that when an extensor muscle contracts, the muscle tone in its opposing flexor muscle is inhibited so that it actively relaxes. In extending the leg, for example, the extensor muscles are put into action and the flexor action is inhibited.

The muscular systems of the body, in fact, are organized in pairs of opposing groups. For example, the pairs of muscles that move the eyes to the right or left react with "reciprocal innervation." Excitation and inhibition are dynamically opposed and both processes are reciprocally related in the simplest of bodily movements.

The integration of positive (excitatory) and negative (inhibitory) hedonic processes* occurs at the higher levels of the central nervous system. This level is above the spinal cord and below the cerebral cortex. At the highest level of the nervous system—the level of the cerebral cortex—there are (as we have seen in the previous section) both inhibitory and excitatory relations between the cortex and lower neural centers. There are diffuse, nonspecific, positive and negative excitations from different receptors. It is clear that these are integrated in the limbic system and lead to a single adaptive reaction of acceptance or rejection.

There is often a *total integration* of an organism's behavior at the cerebral level but occasionally there is more or less *dis*integration. When there is total integration, the organism is free from emotion. A

---

* In the discussion of hedonic integration in Appendix I, positive and negative affective arousals from sensory stimulations are shown to be integrated algebraically so that a single response of acceptance or rejection occurs. There is clearly a reciprocal relationship between positive and negative arousals. In a sense, our findings extend Sherrington's principle of the integrative action of the nervous system.

person can be highly motivated and active in the pursuit of some adaptive activity such as driving to work; his reactions are energetic and free from disturbance. But when purposive activity is frustrated, interrupted, or blocked in any way, there is an affective disturbance. It is such a disturbance that I have defined as emotional.

There are *physiological conflict* theories of emotion. Hodge (1935) pointed out that the brain can respond to a situation through the viscera and/or through the skeletal muscles. When the higher centers of the brain fail to provide a fitting response to the perceived situation or when some doubt, hesitation, or conflict is aroused, there are emotional reactions. *These reactions are inversely proportional to the ability of the higher centers of the brain to meet a given situation.*

A more specific conflict theory of emotion is that of Darrow (1935). He said that because the centers that regulate *excited emotions* are located in the hypothalamus, the role of the cerebral cortex is to (1) differentiate between stimulus patterns, and (2) to maintain an appropriate inhibitory control over subcortical mechanisms of excited response. If circumstances arise which involve a threat to the physical or intellectual equilibrium of an individual, the cortical inhibition is reduced and there is an emotional display. Darrow calls this process "excortication." There is a weakening of cerebral dominance and of total integration during emotional reactions. We say a man has "lost his head" during emotion.

A Comprehensive Account of Feeling and Emotion

Pribram (1967a, 1967b) has formulated an account of emotion based on a thorough analysis of the physiological and neuropsychological facts. In summarizing his view he mentions five points:

1. Emotion is *memory-based* rather than based on drive or visceral processes. In describing emotion one must take account of previous experiences and the present inducing situation. Cognitive processes, including perception, memory, and imagination, play a dominant role in causing emotional behavior.

2. *Organized stability is a baseline from which perturbations occur.* Experiences that differ from the baseline produce a disturbance. An important part of the baseline is the continuous activity of the viscera, regulated through the autonomic nervous system. A mismatch of expected and actual bodily changes in heart rate, sweating, presence of "butterflies," etc., is immediately sensed as a discrepancy. This is the visceral basis of the theories of James and Lange.

3. Emotion is a *perturbation*, an interruption, a disruption of normal

ongoing activity. The theory makes clear the relation between motivation and emotion by linking both to ongoing, prebehavioral organization—i.e., to a plan, program, or disposition. Pribram's theory implies an extension of the homeostatic doctrine from intraorganic events to the dynamic relation between organism and environment. There is behavioral, as well as neural and mental disorganization.

4. Pribram defines emotion as *a process that takes the organism temporarily out of motion* and effects control through the regulation of sensory inputs. The processes that occur when an organism is "out of" or "away from" motion are just as important and interesting scientifically as are the normal activities of an organism carrying out some plan.

5. There is, as noted above, *central control through the regulation of peripheral inputs.* Pribram identifies two forms of regulation of sensory inputs. One form *inhibits* peripheral inputs while the organism determines what to do in a situation, what plan to folllow. The other form *enhances* inputs, thus making the organism attentive to critical aspects of the situation.

In general, Pribram's account of emotion considers the organism as a whole—its perceptions, memories, plans, and the like—in relation to the prevailing environmental situation. This view is closely related to the equilibrium-disequilibrium theories of motivation, in which emotion is seen as a disequilibrium, a perturbation, disturbance, upset.

GENERAL SUMMARY

The complexity of affective processes is so great that studies have necessarily been piecemeal and made from different points of view. An overall view is difficult to gain.

A comprehensive account of feeling and emotion must begin with the fact that simple sensory stimulations have both cognitive (informational) and hedonic (activating) effects. Sensory perception yields information about the outside world; it also yields information about how the world affects the individual. With simple stimulations there are positive (good) and negative (bad) effects.

With the perception of complex environmental situations there are biologically basic meanings: an enemy, a danger, a potential food, a mate, a young one in distress, and so on. Organisms have evolved adaptive responses to biological dangers and opportunities. Other adaptive behavior is learned.

For civilized man, coping with problems that arise in his environment, the situations that produce feelings and emotions are complex. A man may be threatened by bankruptcy or loss of love or by an incurable disease or something else. These situations build up anxiety tension and stress that may erupt into an emotion. We will consider the causes of emotion in Chapter 6.

Emotion is an acute process, an event. This view, however, can be extended to take account of the persisting disturbances which result from conflict, frustration, tension, and stress. When we speak of an emotionally disturbed individual we imply a disturbance that persists through time. Our anxieties, loves, hates, hopes, and resentments stay with us.

5 The Role of Feelings and Emotions in Development

TERMS YOU WILL MEET IN THIS CHAPTER

APPETITIVE BEHAVIOR Behavior in an organism that leads to continuing and repeating the conditions that produced such behavior. Pleasant stimuli lead to appetitive behavior.

AVERSIVE BEHAVIOR Behavior that leads the organism to terminate, escape from, avoid the conditions that elicited this behavior. A painful stimulus leads to aversive behavior.

EXTINCTION The "erasing" of a learned response through disuse or aversive training. (See *Reinforcement.*)

INNATE PERCEPTUAL DISPOSITION Instinctive inclination to react in a particular way to a pattern of stimuli.

LEARNING The process of acquiring certain responses through practice or training.

MOTIVATION, DRIVE An inner impulse that influences the organism to behave in certain purposive, goal-oriented ways.

PREFERENCE An evaluative choice; involves judgment.

REINFORCEMENT The strengthening of the possibility that an organism will continue to react in a particular way to a particular stimulus; implies a learning process. (See *Extinction.*)

In his book about the origin and nature of emotion, the late surgeon G. W. Crile emphasized the role of evolution. He wrote:

When our progenitors came in contact with any exciting element in their environment, action ensued then and there. There was much action—little restraint or emotion. Civilized man is really in auto-captivity. He is subjected to innumerable stimulations, but custom and convention frequently prevent physical action. When these stimulations are sufficiently strong but no action ensues, the reaction constitutes an emotion. A phylogenetic* flight is anger; a phylogenetic flight is fear; a phylogenetic copulation is sexual love, and so one finds in this conception an underlying principle which may be the key to an understanding of the emotions and of certain diseases. (1915, 76)

Man came down from the trees only a relatively short time ago, considering the entire course of organic evolution. Today, while sitting at his desk in command of the complicated machinery of civilization, if he fears a business catastrophe, this fear is manifested in the same physical changes his primitive forebears exhibited in the battle for existence.

Crile also points out that man cannot fear intellectually or dispassionately. Whether the situation that endangers him is a struggle for credit, position, and honor or a physical battle with fists and weapons, he fears with the same vital organs. The inducing situation may be moral, financial, social, or physical, but man's response is a wildly beating heart, accelerated respiration, increased perspiration, trembling, dry mouth, and so forth.

The impulses for defense and escape are born of innumerable injuries which have been inflicted during countless centuries of organic evolution. When the tooth and claw of an enemy sink deeply into unprotected tissue, the deep-lying receptors are stimulated and reflex avoidance is set up at once. Animals that lack escape patterns are likely to be devoured; conversely, those best endowed with injury-avoiding mechanisms are the ones most likely to escape and leave offspring. Thus, Crile concludes, the development of injury-avoiding behavior can be explained in terms of Darwin's "survival of the fittest" principle.

Instinctive Reactions:
Innate Perceptual Dispositions

Nature is full of examples of bodily structures that are well adapted to function: the wings of the bird, the fangs of the reptile, the strong legs of the antelope, and so on. This adaptation of structure to function applies also to the internal organs and especially to the organization of the nervous system. How these beautiful adaptations of structure to function came into being is the story of evolutionary development. It is part of the miracle of life.

Behavior is adapted to the survival of individuals and the species.

* "Phylogenetic" refers to events of evolutionary significance.

The infant responds to painful stimulation by crying; the cry is heard by the mother, who does something about it. The infant stops crying when the nipple is in his mouth, and sucking movements follow instinctively. The nervous system of the baby, indeed, is organized to favor survival. A clear example of this instinctive principle is found in some observations of the ethologist, Tinbergen (1948).

Lorenz and Tinbergen reported some instructive experiments upon the instinctive behavior of birds. They prepared a cardboard silhouette of a flying bird that resembles a swift-moving predatory hawk when moved to the right and a slow-moving harmless goose or other water bird when moved to the left. (See Figure 9.) This figure,

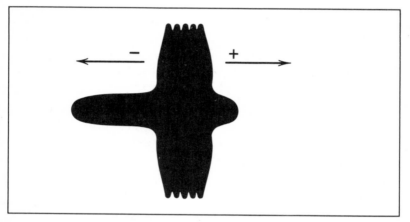

Figure 9. Silhouette of a form that resembles a hawk when moved to the right and a harmless goose when moved to the left. After Tinbergen (1948).

appropriately suspended on wires, caused fear in certain species of birds when it moved in the hawklike direction, but it elicited little more than passive attention when moving in the gooselike direction.

The discrimination appeared in several species of birds reared in captivity. It depends upon a combination of two visual characters, outline and movement. The facts clearly indicate that an innate perceptual disposition underlies this discrimination. The biological utility of such a discrimination is obvious.

In this connection, Troland (1938) formulated a theory of motivation and emotion for which he coined the following terms:

Beneception—A process in a sense organ or afferent nerve channel that is indicative of conditions or events that are typically beneficial to the individual or species.

Nociception—A process in a sense organ or afferent nerve channel that is indicative of conditions or events that are typically injurious to the individual or species.

Neutroception—Any kind of sensory process that is neither beneceptive or nociceptive.

As examples of beneception, Troland named erotic excitation; taste (gustatory) stimulation from sugars (carbohydrate substances furnish fuel for muscular activity); smelling (olfactory) responses to the odors which are indicative of the presence of fresh vegetable products useful as food; the tactual feeling of warmth which indicates the proximity of heat energy needed in cold environments to restore or maintain temperature equilibrium of the body. The following are examples of nociception: pain excitation from damaged tissues; intraorganic stimulations from such bodily conditions as hunger, excessive heat or cold; need for air or water; need to urinate or defecate; bitter tastes, foul odors, etc. These bodily stimulations indicate conditions which are detrimental to the organism or the species. Finally, neutroceptive processes were illustrated by sensory reactions—neither beneficial nor harmful—which occur in perceiving weak noises, colors of medium brilliance, indifferent odors, and so on. Much observant and manipulative behavior (curiosity) is neutroceptive, as we have mentioned earlier.

Troland's criterion of beneception and nociception is *biological.* Organisms have evolved in such a way that in the long run their behavior furthers survival of individual and species. How this has come about is the fascinating story (and mystery) of evolution.

Troland's work implies instinctive dispositions to react positively or negatively to a wide variety of stimulus situations. Beneceptive perception is typically, not invariably, pleasant. Nociceptive perception is typically, not invariably, unpleasant. But Troland's criteria are *biological* and not subjective feelings.

LIKING AND DISLIKING:
THE DEVELOPMENT OF APPETITIVE AND AVERSIVE BEHAVIOR

In earlier chapters we have seen that behind every act of perceiving lies the individual's past history and experience. A cognitive organization is developed within a person that determines how he will react to certain stimuli. These stimuli may come from the outside environment (a sudden chilly breeze) or from within the body (a feeling of hunger). Certain behavior patterns, attitudes, habits, judgments, opinions, ways of reacting to things, and so forth develop within all of us as a result of our past experience. It is not difficult to understand how a child who has consistently been punished by being forced to stay in a dark closet can develop a loathing, and even a fear, of dark and small places. The vegetarian from India may feel nauseous when he observes an American child gobbling a juicy red hamburger. Putting it into more scientific terminology, we can say that the social conditions in that Indian's life led him to perceive raw meat in a hedonically negative way. A Vermont Yankee might find humid weather ennervating, while a Georgia resident might feel the same about a cool, snowy day. Positive and negative feelings—or pleasant and unpleasant sensations —are partly a result of innate biological predispositions (a lighted match will make almost anyone yelp with pain) and partly a result of conditioning, learning.

Thus it is clear that sensory stimulations elicit positive, negative, and hedonically neutral effects. Positive effects are *appetitive* in that they lead the organism to continue and repeat the conditions producing them. Negative effects are *aversive* in that they lead the organism to terminate, escape from, and avoid the conditions that elicit them. Many stimulus patterns are hedonically *neutral;* they are found in observant, exploratory, and manipulative behavior.

Hedonic effects occur not only with sensory stimulations from outside the body but also with deep-lying intraorganic excitations and conditions. There are uncomfortable pains and aches arising from disturbances of homeostasis and from diseases. There are also the positive comforts of dietary satisfaction, sex, health, and well-being.

These *primary affective arousals* play a dominant role in the organization and development of appetitive and aversive behavior. In Appendix I, I have described some experiments with rats that show the role of hedonic processes in behavioral development. These experiments show that pleasure and unpleasure control the growth of appetites and aversions. The work has human importance because it helps us understand how food preferences, aversions, and addictions develop. A person may be "hooked" on cigarettes or marijuana or alcohol. It is not easy to get off the hook because a tolerance for these drugs has been developed. But in the development of these addictions, pleasure, and especially the relief from unpleasure, plays an important part. An addiction, however, differs from a simple motor habit (such as typewriting) in that it involves a biochemical adaptation of the body to intake of the drug.

Development of Preferences

A distinction can be drawn between *sensory* and *preferential* discrimination. You can easily discriminate between black and white or between sweet and bitter tastes; these discriminations are *sensory*, not preferential. But when you report that a sweet taste is more pleasant, more desirable than a bitter taste, you are making an *evaluative discrimination*. A preference is here defined as an *evaluative choice*. With human beings, the pleasantness or unpleasantness of contact with a particular stimulus determines acceptance, rejection, and preference. There are also delayed hedonic effects, as well as immediate effects, that influence human preferences. Feelings of comfort and discomfort follow the ingestion of certain foods. We are all familiar with the "green apple" effect!

Making and Breaking Habits:
Reinforcement and Extinction

Through what mechanisms do we learn appetitive and aversive behavior? What does all this have to do with our feelings and emotions? We have seen that the *effect* of a particular stimulus (hunger pangs, the taste of salt, a picture of a rainbow, the sound of a fingernail being scraped on a blackboard) is pleasant, unpleasant, or hedonically neutral. How is it that we develop these perceptions? It is here that the concepts of *reinforcement* and *extinction* are important. Reinforcement can be defined as an increase in the probability that a repeated stimulus situation will elicit a specific response. Extinction is a decrease in this probability.

Reference to the studies described in Appendix I will show that there can be a growth of preferential discrimination between a pair of test foods. This depends upon two interrelated factors: (1) hedonic processes—the relative palatability of the test foods; and (2) exercise—the frequency of repetition of a choice. The first of these factors is motivational; the second implies a process of learning.

Thorndike long ago described two basic laws of learning: the law of exercise and the law of effect. There can be no doubt about the importance of these two factors but, as a matter of logic, it would be better to specify them as laws of *development*. Then *learning* could be defined as an increase in probability due to exercise (practice, training); extinction, as a decrease in probability due to disuse. Extinction, whether or not we regard it as a fact of learning, depends upon the same two factors: affective arousal and repetition of response.

In addition to the factors of learning and motivation there is also a third important factor in development: maturation or growth. Many instinctive reactions of organisms are present at birth or develop subsequently during some stages of growth. They are not learned but depend upon millions of years of evolution. Also they develop with exercise. For example, the development of walking in the infant depends upon age. Incidentally, the child appears to have pleasure in taking the first steps. He is encouraged by his parents in "learning" to walk.

Hedonic changes are important factors at all stages of development. Those toward the positive and away from the negative tend to be repeated. Conversely, hedonic changes away from the positive and toward the negative tend to be inhibited or extinguished. Perhaps we should say that *reactions that produce hedonic changes in the positive direction are learned; those that produce hedonic changes in the negative direction are inhibited or extinguished.* There is thus an hedonic basis for the organization of appetitive and aversive behavior.

We should also remember that there are neutral forms of regulation and learning. Once a habit has been organized and exercised, it has an existence that is independent of positive and negative hedonic effects. A habit organization may be activated quite apart from hedonic effects. Motives, plans, and intentions can utilize latent habit organizations to arrive at some goal. For example, a thirsty animal *learns* to make a long trek to the water hole. It is doubtlessly uncomfortable, and will act to relieve or remove that discomfort. But even if thirst is negligible, an animal will join others in a trek to the water hole. Habit organization dominates the purposive behavior.

I will speculate that an animal joining others on a trek to the water hole has a *cognitive expectation* which might be formulated in human terms as "finding water" or "relieving thirst." Unfortunately, animals can't talk. But their behavior communicates an expectation.*

Motivation:
Hedonic Processes and Drive

In the natural world there are many examples of persistent goal-oriented behavior, such as birds, which migrate to avoid the extremes of winter, and cattle, which travel for miles to reach the salt licks.

---

* C. L. Trafton's experiment with affective arousal and development of cognitive expectations, as reported in Young (1966, p. 79), is included, for the interested reader, in Appendix I.

And in the laboratory you can observe the development of purposive, goal-oriented, behavior. The rat learns to find his way through the maze to food in the goal box; he develops a behavioral drive. He also *learns* to avoid the grill that has yielded painful shocks.

What is this drive, or motivation, underlying persisting approach and avoidance behavior? How does such behavior develop, come into being?

According to Hull's drive-reduction theory of motivation, there is a persisting drive stimulus from tissues in need. For example, deprivation of water produces a condition of thirst with persisting internal stimulation. The reduction or removal of this stimulation "reinforces" the reactions that lead to drive-stimulus reduction. Through drive reduction, goal-directed habits develop. The habit is directive; the stimulus, motivating.

Spence, Logan, and other neo-Hullian theorists, have emphasized incentive motivation that has positive and negative aspects. Their research ties in nicely with hedonic theory.

According to hedonic theory, stimulation has both informational and activating aspects. Some stimuli are positively activating and lead to the organization of appetitive behavior. Others are negatively activating and lead to the organization and repetition of aversive behavior. This is the basis for formation of habits of seeking and withdrawing.

Appetite, Aversion, and Disgust

Universal habits of food seeking are motivated by the physiological state of hunger. The specific techniques of acquiring food obviously vary from species to species. The spider patiently awaits the fly's landing on the sticky web. The hungry cat may leap onto the counter to steal the lamb chop. You and I go to the refrigerator. To some extent these techniques develop through a process of learning. At all stages of development, however, food-seeking behavior is regulated by the interaction of physiological drive and environmental situations. The satisfaction of hunger reinforces patterns of behavior that lead to obtaining and eating food.

The internal state of hunger can be distinguished from appetite. Hunger is experienced as a gnawing sensation in the stomach. Appetite is a conscious desire for food which may exist in the absence of hunger. Salted nuts and other tidbits are called "appetizers" because they build up a desire to eat.

On the negative side of the feeding process there are two phases.

Stimulation of the senses of smell, touch, or taste may bring immediate aversion. Bitter and sour tastes, foul odors, and painful temperatures bring a prompt rejection of the food object. Distinct from this aversion is an intraorganic rejection which is shown by retching and vomiting. There may be feelings of nausea and sickishness. Darwin pointed out long ago that the facial expression of disgust is that of a person preparing to vomit.

I recall that as a boy I walked through a vacant lot and came across the body of a rabbit covered with maggots and giving off the strong odor of decaying flesh. The experience was so sickening that I retched. For months after this experience I kept away from the spot where the dead rabbit had been found and when possible avoided going through the vacant lot.

The question "What disgusts us?" literally means "What environmental conditions, perceived or remembered, induce the nausea-vomiting pattern of response?" To many people it is disgusting to find a fly in milk or a hair on butter. Perhaps there is the thought that these things contaminate food and might be eaten.

In common language, however, the term *disgust* refers to almost any kind of loathing or aversion rather than to a specific pattern of vomiting. Thus a hetereosexual person might be "disgusted" by overt homosexual activities. Or a clergyman may be "disgusted" by a TV show that features violence and inhumanity. The revulsion or strong dislike is entirely free from the nausea-vomiting pattern.

EMOTIONAL DEVELOPMENT IN THE CHILD

In an extended series of observations, Bridges (1930, 1931, 1932) described the different forms of emotional behavior that arise during the first two years of human life. She approached the study with no bias concerning the nature of emotion, assuming that everyone knows what an emotion is. Her subjects were infants in the Montreal Foundling and Baby Hospital and in a nursery school.

According to Bridges, the infant's first emotional response is a general agitation produced by various stimulating conditions. Diffuse excitement is an innate emotional reaction—perhaps the only general one. During emotional excitement in the baby, arms and hand muscles are tensed, breath is quickened, legs make jerky kicking movements, eyes are opened as if gazing into the distance, with the upper lid arched. Some of the stimulations that produce such agitation are direct sunlight in the infant's eyes, suddenly picking up the infant and putting him down, pulling the infant's arm through the dress sleeve, holding arms tightly to the side, the noisy clatter of a something thrown onto metal, and so on.

It is difficult, Bridges observed, to distinguish between diffuse emotional excitement and distress and negative emotion; but in a three-week-old infant, *excitement* and *distress* are definitely distinguishable.

The cry of distress in the month-old baby is irregular. There are short intakes of breath and long cries of expiration. The eyes are "screwed up" tight, the face is flushed, fists are often clenched, the arms are tense, and legs are still or kicking spasmodically. The mouth is open and square- or kidney-shaped with the corners pulled down. The pitch of the cry is high, and the sounds something like "ah, cu-ah, cu-ah, cu-aeh." (See Figure 2, page 15.)

Cries of distress were heard from month-old babies on waking suddenly from sleep, struggling to breathe through nostrils blocked with mucus, when ears were discharging, when lying awake before feeding time, after staying long in the same position, lying on a wet diaper when the buttocks were chafed, and when the fingers were rapped. The three main causes of distress at this age are discomfort, pain, and hunger.

According to Bridges, then, the first emotional behavior observable in the infant is a diffuse and neutral *excitement* that depends upon various kinds of stimulation. During the first few weeks *distress*, or negative emotional excitement, can be distinguished from the primal form of excitement. Bridges regards the birth cry as a reflex incidental to the establishment of respiration; it can be distinguished from the cry of distress.

The response of *delight*, or positive emotional excitement, appears after *distress*, usually before the third month of life. Delight is shown by smiles, laughs, coos, and gurgles. At eight months of age the child seems to take delight in self-initiated purposeful activity. He babbles and splutters and laughs to himself. He seems delighted with the noise he makes by banging spoons and other playthings on the table. Throwing things from the crib brings delight. He waves, pats, and coos, drawing in long breaths, when familiar adults swing him or talk to him. He watches the person who nurses him attentively, exploring her, patting gently, often smiling. Here are perhaps the first demonstrations of affection. The child will also smile at his mirror image; but this behavior is inquisitive rather than affectionate.

More specific forms of emotional behavior develop during the first two years of life. Bridges prepared a schedule of emotional development based on her observations (Figure 10); she discusses in detail the gradual growth of specific forms of emotional behavior.

The specific emotions, then, develop out of a primary excitement. The primitive forms of emotional behavior are positive and negative. But there is a primary form of neutral excitement, or activation, that is present at birth and persists during the first two years and, in fact, throughout the life span.

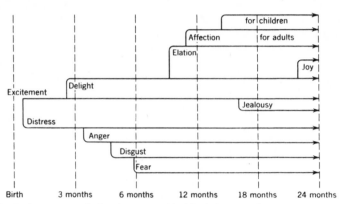

Figure 10. Early emotional development. Modified from Bridges (1932). The diagram shows approximate ages at which different emotions emerge from more primitive forms during the first two years of life.

Bridges points out that emotional development and social development go hand in hand and are intimately connected. In fact emotional development might well be treated as an aspect of social development.

General characteristics of emotional development are: (1) decreasing frequency of intense emotional responses; (2) progressive transfer of emotional responses to situations that are socially approved; and (3) gradual changes in the nature of overt emotional responses in accordance with training and social pressures.

Development of Anger

In a careful study of the development of anger in young children, Goodenough (1931) trained college-educated mothers to observe and record outbursts of anger in their children. Attention was paid to the causes of anger, the manifestations, the duration, the time of occurrence, and other details. Forty-five children, from 7 months to 7 years and 10 months, were observed. There were 2,124 recorded outbursts of anger.

In the early stages of development there was a random display of undirected energy, including jumping up and down, holding the breath, stamping, kicking, throwing self on the floor, pouting, screaming, etc.

In later stages, there was retaliative behavior. It took the form of throwing objects, grabbing, pinching, biting, striking, calling names, arguing and insisting, breaking things, etc. The form of retaliative behavior was found to depend somewhat upon the age of the child. A small child may bite when frustrated; an older child may strike or throw something at the offender. Still older children retaliate verbally, but the size of a child's vocabulary varies with age and experience. A youth or adult may plot revenge or seek retributive justice, to "get even."

Table 1 shows clearly the transition from undirected energy

TABLE 1

Age in years	0–1	1–2	2–3	3–4	4–8
Percentages of outbursts with undirected energy					
Boys	100.0	78.0	73.1	65.2	34.0
Girls	86.0	78.7	83.3	29.6	29.0
Both	88.9	78.4	75.1	59.9	36.3
Percentages of outbursts with retaliative behavior					
Boys	0.0	9.4	10.4	25.7	30.0
Girls	0.8	3.8	11.5	25.3	36.3
Both	0.7	6.3	10.6	25.6	28.0

Data from Goodenough (1931).

outbursts to retaliative behavior as age advances. Emotional development goes from undirected displays of energy to behavior that becomes increasingly retaliative, hostile, and aggressive.

In anger there is an impulse to destroy whatever blocks purposive behavior. With adults, however, hostility is often suppressed and not openly manifested as it is with small children. Suppressed hostility commonly leads to displaced aggression.

Development of Fear

Reactions of caution and fear are widespread throughout nature. They have an obvious protective function in the face of potential danger as, for example, in avoiding predators.

In Hebb's (1946) investigation of the kinds of objects and situations that elicit fear in chimpanzees, he exposed a test object for thirty seconds while observing the behavior of the animal in its presence. The objects that most frequently excited fear in the chimps were a skull with moving jaw, a painted wax snake, the moving head of a monkey, a plaster cast of a chimpanzee face, and a human head. It is well known that chimpanzees fear toy animals and snakes, but the observation of fear of parts of chimpanzees' and human bodies was new. The sight of a clay chimpanzee head, when carried from cage to cage, produced avoidance akin to panic in five or six of the thirty test animals.

Behavioral criteria used in determining the presence of fear were: (1) consistent withdrawal that continues when the position of the test object is changed; (2) withdrawing behavior appearing abruptly when the test object is presented; (3) coincident excitation, such as erection of hair, screaming, threatening gestures directed at the test object, or continued orientation of the gaze at the object while the animal is moving directly away from it.

Hebb pointed out that fear comes about spontaneously; the animals did not have to learn the fear responses. The evidence indicates that fear, in both man and chimpanzee, occurs spontaneously when the subject is presented with mutilated and unresponsive bodies. Other investigators have shown that fear is produced by situations that are strange, not well understood. The fear of strangers must be based upon an *experienced discrepancy* rather than upon some property of the sensory excitation; the discrepancy is relative to previous experience.

The child, like the chimpanzee, responds innately with fear to sudden and unexpected stimulations: to loud sounds, falling, sudden movement, and other abrupt changes in stimulation. But the response to strangers and unfamiliar features of the environment changes with age and experience.

Jersild and Holmes (1935) studied the kinds of situations that elicit fear in children of different ages. A general finding was that the frequency of specific fears varies markedly with age. Some of the results are shown graphically in Figure 11. This figure is based upon records kept by parents over a twenty-one-day period. In the study, 953 fear-inducing situations were recorded.

Some fear-inducing situations decrease in effectiveness with age; others increase. The curves at the left show examples of fear-inducing situations that decrease in frequency and effectiveness from ages 1 to 6. The curves at the right show fear-inducing situations that increase.

These changes are doubtless due to the child's increasing understanding and control of the environment. As he or she develops, experience teaches the child what kinds of objects and situations to fear and avoid.

Development of Smiling and Laughing

The smiling response is usually absent at birth; it normally appears during the third to sixth month of life. Like many other reflexes of the infant, smiling is not rigidly attached to a fixed pattern of stimulation but is elicited by a variety of stimulations.

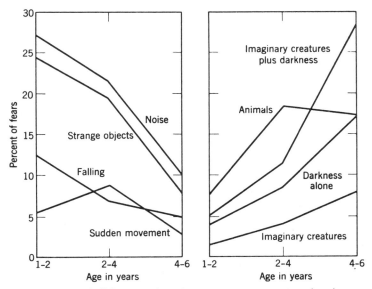

Figure 11. Percentage of all fears attributed to various situations as related to age. After Jersild and Holmes (1935).

By the age of six months the smile becomes a normal response to social stimulation. Charlotte Bühler believes that smiling is a specific response of the infant to social contacts, to the appearance and voice of a human being. Arnold Gesell, however, believes that the smile is an innate mark of satisfaction resulting from being fed and placed in a warm crib; the response becomes conditioned to the mother's face and to social situations by repeated satisfactions. Social stimulation, then, through conditioning, comes to elicit a response that was originally elicited by nonsocial stimulation.

The development of smiling during the first year of life was investigated by Spitz (1946). He repeatedly observed 251 randomly selected infants of different races and different environments. To elicit smiling, he applied several kinds of stimulation. In one group of experiments the experimenter turned his face to the infant so that a smiling mouth and both eyes could be seen simultaneously. If the infant smiled, the experimenter turned his face slowly into profile, continuing either to smile or nod. Spitz found that the human face, presented in front view, elicited smiling when the infants were three to six months of age.

Other experiments were made with masks and puppets. On the basis of many observations, Spitz concluded that it is *not* the human face, as such, that elicits smiling, but a configuration of elements in the facial stimulus pattern. The configuration consists of two eyes presented front face, combined with a factor of motion. The motion can be produced by nodding or by moving various facial muscles (sticking out the tongue through the mask).

Spitz confirmed the finding of other investigators that the smile in response to a particular stimulus is absent during the first 20 days of life and rarely appears during the first 60 days. The pattern normally matures during the third to sixth months. Spitz reported that smiling in response to the above stimulations disappears after the sixth month; but it reappears and is complete by the end of the eighth month. The reason for this temporary disappearance is not clear.

Smiling and laughing are normally elicited in *social* situations. Kenderdine (1931), in her study of laughter in the preschool child, reported that out of 223 situations in which laughter was observed, only 14 or 6.3 percent occurred when the child was alone. The presence of other persons seems to be an essential element in the occurrence of laughter in children, although the mere presence of others does not mean that there will necessarily be an increased amount of laughter.

Kenderdine found that preschool children laughed most frequently in situations that involved motions made by the child himself or by other persons or by toys. Next in effectiveness were situations regarded as socially unacceptable, such as kicking a person, belching, or other "bad manners." Third were situations in which an element of humor was appreciated, as in a joke.

Smiling and laughing are typically pleasant, hedonically positive. So also is the free play of children and, apparently, the play of animals. The young and immature of many animal forms play in different ways, but all seem to "enjoy" the process.

Development of Sexual Behavior and Feelings

In human development there are marked physical and mental changes that go along with the process of maturation. Hormones are produced in the cells of the body, especially in the ductless glands. These substances are circulated to all parts of the body. They influence growth, metabolism, reproduction, activity, and vigor.

Especially important as determinants of growth and behavior are secretions from the gonads (reproductive glands) and the pituitary body. The testis of the male, in addition to forming sperm cells that carry the paternal chromosomes, secretes hormones directly into the blood. The ovary of the female, in addition to forming egg cells that carry the maternal chromosomes, pours out hormones into the blood stream. These hormones regulate growth and influence sexual behavior. The pituitary gland the gonads act reciprocally. The secretions of the pituitary stimulate gonadal secretion which, in turn, acts to check the pituitary secretion.

Some of the changes associated with increased activity of the testis are shown in Figure 12, which is based upon the report of Kinsey et al. (1948). Between the ages of 12 and 15, most boys go through a period of rapid growth with voracious eating. Pubic hair appears, the beard begins to grow, the voice lowers, and there is rapid increase in stature. Sex interest and sex activity are stepped up until, within a few years, most young men reach their maximal rate of sexual activity.

Equivalent changes—pubic hair, breast development, rapid growth, etc.—occur at puberty with the female, but at a slightly earlier age.

In a multidisciplinary account of sexual motivation and feeling, K. R. Hardy (1964, 1965) formulated a theory of sexual development in which hedonic processes and expectations of pleasing effects play a dominant role. Hardy agrees with F. A. Beach that the prevailing doctrine of sexual motivation, based on analogy with the hunger and

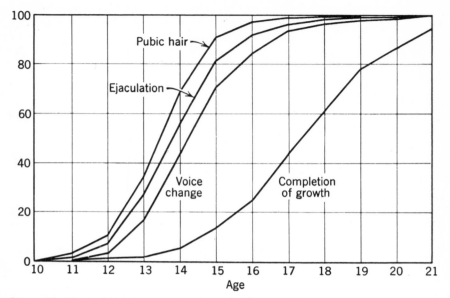

Figure 12. Physical developments in the male during adolescence. After Kinsey et al. (1948). The curves show age at which pubic hair appears; age of first ejaculation; age at which voice changes; age upon completion of growth.

thirst drives, is inadequate. Hormones and physiological tensions are assuredly important motivations, but these factors do not completely explain the complex facts of human sexual behavior.

Hardy stated some general principles of motivation and emphasized the importance of pleasantness from tactile and specifically from genital stimulations in organizing and developing positive appetitive behavior. He pointed out that when stimulus cues are repeatedly associated with pleasantness, these cues arouse an expectation of positive hedonic effects. Specific forms of sexual behavior—masturbation, intercourse, animal contacts, and others—appear to be organized and to develop on the basis of hedonic effects from sensory stimulations.

The doctrine of expectation based on habituation to hedonic effects provides a sound basis for understanding the growth and continuance of sexual habits and appetites. Hardy takes account of the habituation effect in relation to sexual appetites. With repetition, both positive and negative hedonic effects develop stable dispositions which tend to become autonomous (self-determined) and, moreover, lead to expectation of further hedonic effects.

Hardy also considers cultural and social factors, and differences in sexual codes and mores. Negative hedonic effects are derived from the frustration of sexual motives and from conflicts. What this means is that the girl who never has a date begins to doubt her feminine appeal. The boy who is shorter than all the girls in his class may develop a woman-hating attitude as a defense. Such negative effects involve a conflict between approaching and avoiding a person of the opposite sex.

Hardy's cogent analysis of sexual motivation is, I believe, more realistic than Freud's doctrines of the libido and sublimation of an instinctive drive. The extension of hedonic theory into the realm of sexual motivation is worthy of careful consideration by psychologists. The human problems of living, of course, involve more than sex and the search for happiness.

EMOTIONAL MATURITY AND CONTROL

As a person advances from infancy to adult life, the characteristics of his emotional behavior change radically. The change comes with growth and maturation of bodily structures; with experience and the process of learning; with the ever-changing environmental situation; and especially with social and interpersonal relations. When emotional development reaches a certain stage, we say that the person is emotionally mature.

However, not everyone has the same development. Not everyone achieves emotional maturity. The person who as a small child got his way by kicking and screaming usually learns better ways of persuading. This is a result of his growth, the influence of his parents and his peers, and so forth. It is not to say, however, that everyone uses increasingly rational and mature ways of dealing with life situations. We all know someone who throws the equivalent of childhood tantrums when he or she is frustrated. John kicks the dog, Mary Ann throws dishes, and Fred bites his nails. In fact, we all resort to more or less juvenile behavior once in a while. But on the whole, "well-adjusted" people learn to control their emotions to a certain extent. Some control them too much. Chris never seems to show any emotions—friends call her a "cold fish," but she longs to learn how to respond more warmly to people and situations. Jay's parents were quiet people who paid only minimal, though decent, attention to their children—thus he feels he comes across as a dry, uninteresting person.

He cannot make close friends, and though he performs adequately in his life situations, he senses a lack of passion and color.

Both extremes—overcontrol and lack of emotional control—result from the individual differences in a person's growth, his learning, his experiences. How can we become "emotionally mature"? Is it possible to *learn* how to be mature? Can an adult change his personality, his ways of responding to life, his emotional makeup? These are but a few of the questions that concern most people interested in feelings and emotions.

Emotional Maturity and Immaturity

What is emotional maturity? When is a person emotionally grown up? These questions have not been answered satisfactorily because psychologists do not agree as to how the concept of *emotion* should be defined. Further, there is a lack of sound experimental data.

According to Hollingsworth (1928) and Morgan (1934), the best way to approximate the meaning of *emotional maturity* is to note the changes in emotional behavior that take place as a child develops into an adult and to contrast the emotional responses of children with those of adults. The following account is based on the analyses of Hollingsworth and Morgan.

An important contrast between the emotional behavior of infant, young child, and adult is in the *degree of frustration tolerance.* The infant does not tolerate discomfort and thwarting. Hunger pains, a bath that is too cold or too warm, the prick of a pin, restraint of free movement, unfamiliar sounds—all these arouse an emotional display in the infant. The older child is more tolerant of frustration. Instead of crying like a baby at every mishap, he withstands suffering and disappointment with fewer signs of disturbance.

A two-year-old kicks and screams when refused a second helping of some desired food. Adults take this for granted. They say, "He is just a baby and he behaves like one emotionally." If, however, a six-year-old behaves in the same manner, he is regarded as "naughty." When a nine-year-old kicks and screams in this situation we say he is "spoiled." But such conduct from an adult would be regarded as a sign of emotional immaturity. If an adult were to scream and kick because he or she was refused a second helping at dinner, a psychiatrist would be summoned!

In the ancient pubertal ceremonies of a certain primitive people, physical and mental hardships were inflicted as an ordeal, to introduce the youth to adulthood. If the youth refused to submit to the ordeal or yielded to the grilling situation with outcries of fear or distress, he failed in his initiation to adulthood. Some traces of this custom may remain in the occasional fraternity initiation. Thus, a capacity to endure pain and to face danger with fortitude is often considered a criterion of emotional maturity.

A second contrast between the emotional behavior of child and adult is a *decrease in frequency and degree of emotional upset* as the individual grows up. An adult does not display an outburst of anger as frequently as a child, nor does he weep so often. When the adult is emotionally aroused, his response is less intense than that of a child. If an adult pinches his fingers, he does not scream as loudly as possible—he yells at a level that is consistent with his age, the situation, the time, the place, etc.—that is, he uses judgment in his response. (Alone, I may curse and grimace and leap when I hammer my thumb instead of the nail. But if my minister or teacher or daughter is nearby, I am apt to moderate my observable response.)

On the physiological level, it can be said that the adult manifests a higher degree of cerebral control over subcortical arousals than does the child. This is largely the result of social training and experience. Present-day American culture (perhaps wrongly) discourages overt expressions of weeping, anger, fear, and encourages, or at least does not discourage, smiling and laughing. But on those rare occasions when an adult is genuinely horrified, terrified, or enraged, emotional outbursts may occur with all their primitive intensity. Some reactions seem almost instinctive. It must not be concluded that the adult, in our civilization, has lost a capacity for emotional outbursts but only that under usual conditions he is better controlled by his cerebral machinery than the child. The cerebral control of the adult is such that what we call "emotional behavior" is less likely to arise than with children.

There is also another factor. The adult commonly suppresses the outward manifestations of emotion. On this account he reveals emotion overtly with less frequency than does the child.

A third contrast between child and adult is a difference in the *impulsiveness or explosiveness of behavior.* The child "cannot wait" to express anger, joy, or fear. He must respond without delay. In anger he bites or strikes; in joy, jumps up and down, claps his hands, laughs; in fear, he cries out or runs away; in pain he cries and screams. The adult, in contrast, is usually able to delay his response and manifests less impulsiveness.

A fourth difference between the emotional behavior of child and adult is found in the *attitudes of self-regard.* Injury to the human ego awakens in the child a self-pity that is out of proportion to the pity felt by sympathetic onlookers and comforters. This solicitude for the self is keenly felt by the injured person.

Writes Hollingworth:

> In childhood self-pity is unrestrained. The injury to the person strikes at the very center of the universe. The mature person approximates the "poor-you" attitude in pitying his own injuries and mishaps. He tries to feel no sorrier for himself than others would feel for him, and strives against sinking into the "poor-me" attitude, with its childish appeal for sympathy from others which they cannot sincerely give. The emotionally mature person does not prey upon the amiability of his fellow men. (210)

This self-pity of the child reflects the fact that he is self-centered. As his knowledge of the world increases, he becomes less obviously egocentric. This may be due to the fact that excessive manifestations of self-interest are commonly disapproved. Signs of self-pity are suppressed more in adults than in children. Although most adults are self-centered and concerned about their individual welfare, their self-interest is commonly camouflaged. There is a great deal of current literature that actually encourages overt expression and recognition of "basic" emotions, however. Many psychologists feel that men in our society, for example, are wrongly discouraged from weeping. Self-control, in many cases, is increasingly seen as denial of honest feelings and emotions. It is a fact that the person who suffers many frustrations without "blowing off steam" fairly regularly may be increasing his or her chances of developing ulcers. Recognition of interest in oneself is seen by many to be the key to successful understanding of and relationships with others.

Finally, in today's world, *the child, in contrast with the adult, is more overt in his emotional manifestations.* If an adult is grieved, he refrains from weeping; if angered, he controls the facial muscles which express anger and an impulse to attack; if afraid, he assumes the anti-fear attitude of courage. Thus, although he may experience an emotion, he inhibits its outward manifestation. The child, in contrast, is usually overt, direct, and quite frank in his emotional behavior. How many times have parents of small children witnessed the following kind of a scene!

Jo: Mama! Bobbi kicked me and hit me, for nothing. Boo-hoo, boo-hoo!
Bobbi: Jo hit me first and I only got even!
Jo: Mama! Bobbi kicked me and hit me and took my crayons away. That's bad! Boo-hoo, boo-hoo!
Bobbi: I don't care! So there! (strikes)

Throughout this little drama there is the greatest openness of emotional demonstration. Compare it with the "silent treatment" a husband and wife may exhibit after an argument.

Summing up, it can be said that the child in contrast with the adult is generally (1) less tolerant of discomfort and thwarting; (2) given to more frequent and intense outbursts of emotion; (3) more impulsive, explosive in behavior, and with less capacity to delay responses; (4) more given to self-pity and egocentricity; (5) more overt and frank in emotional displays.

Emotional Control

In discussing the dimensions of affective arousal, we have talked about *the level of total integration or degree of cerebral control.* This is an important dimension for the definition of emotion. (See page 25.)

The total response of an individual to an environmental situation, though highly visceralized, can remain integrated and free from signs of outer disturbance. When a person has understanding and knowledge of a situation and skill in coping with it, emotional upset does not necessarily arise. *It is the lack of ability to cope adequately with the environment that produces emotion.*

To illustrate: A five-year-old boy was afraid to go to bed at night. There were threatening shadows moving on the wall of his bedroom. His father explained that the shadows were cast by branches moving in front of a street light. The child was shown the branches moving in the wind. He was allowed to produce other shadows by moving the window curtains. When the boy understood the cause of the shadows and could produce them himself, his fear vanished. The fear came from lack of understanding and inability to control the situation.

According to a common meaning of *emotional control,* an emotion may still be present when the outward manifestations of disturbance are voluntarily suppressed. Thus, a man may control his words and actions but he may blush involuntarily, in embarrassment. Control is limited to the somatic mechanisms: to facial expression, vocalization, gesture, and ways of acting. Current research, however, indicates that we can in fact gain control of such "involuntary" processes as heart beat, blood pressure, glandular secretions. Consider the Indian mystic who develops, through training, a breath control that allows him to remain under the earth for long periods of time. Also relevant are the contemporary studies of people who have learned the techniques of TM—transcendental meditation—and who, during meditation, exhibit a physiological state in which brain waves show undeniable calm. And consider the concentration and control needed by the life of the party when he whistles "Yankee Doodle" while a friend sucks a lemon!

The voluntary enactment of emotional behavior does not necessarily induce visceral responses. Years ago William James interviewed actors, asking whether they *felt* the emotions they enacted on the stage. Testimony was sharply divided: some actors said they did and others said that they did not *feel* the emotions they expressed. Perhaps some actors played the emotional role as an art with their skeletal musculature. Others threw themselves into the part, identifying themselves empathically with the character and the situation and allowing the response to become visceralized.

If emotion is defined as an affective disturbance, an upset, disruption, perturbation, turbulence, etc., arising from a psychological situation, then a reaction is emotional to the extent that such affective disorganization is present. Purposive behavior with complete cerebral control may be highly motivated, adaptive, and biologically serviceable, but by definition it is not necessarily *emotional*. Complete control, however, is frequently lacking. And the affective disturbance constitutes an acute emotion.

When all is said and done, it remains obvious that individuals differ in the nature and degree of their emotional control. There are, for example, differences in frustration tolerance. An insult may throw one person into a fuming rage and leave another unperturbed.

Pathological states induced by drugs, in psychoses, under great stress, and similar conditions can result in dyscontrol with loss of sanity and rationality. Emotional dyscontrol is indicated by criminal acts such as murder, rape, violent attack, and other behaviors. When such reactions occur, the help of a psychiatrist is needed.

The Course of Emotional Development

There is a normal course of development from emotional upset to adaptive behavior. This is beautifully illustrated by an experiment on aversive conditioning. The experiment, illustrated by a film, was performed by the late E. K. Culler; it dealt with auditory sensitivity of the dog.*

A dog was harnessed to an apparatus that delivered a painful shock to its foot a few seconds after an auditory signal, a tone. If the animal lifted his foot from the grid, he could avoid the shock.

---

* The film, entitled *Motor Conditioning in Dogs*, was prepared by Professor Culler in the Animal Hearing Laboratory at the University of Illinois. The film is distributed by the C. H. Stoelting Company, 1350 S. Kostner Ave., Chicago, Ill. 60623.

On the first trial a tone was sounded and the shock followed. When stimulated painfully on the foot, the animal struggled, yelped, bit the apparatus, and was highly excited. In this agitated state the foot was raised from the grid and the painful stimulation stopped. With repeated stimulations, the foot was raised more and more promptly and the emotional agitation was lessened. Finally, there was a calm, adaptive raising of the foot when the tone sounded, and no emotion was exhibited. The animal was now conditioned and ready for the auditory experiment. Raising the foot was a signal that the animal responded to the tone. The course of emotional development in this case was from emotional excitement to calm, nonemotional, behavior.

With human subjects, emotional development is shown by an increasing ability to cope with problems so that emotional disturbances do not arise. The emotionally mature individual is said to be integrated at the highest neural level. But in everyday life complete integration develops gradually with experience. We are never completely free from feelings and emotional problems. Nor can we expect to be! An integrated outlook on life does not necessarily imply complete control. A person who is intellectually and physically mature and who has a realistic outlook on life will still react emotionally from time to time. He will weep when someone he loves dies. He will swear when insulted by a rival. He will laugh at a joke. These emotional reactions relieve tension and help to bring a return to a person's normal mood and composure.

Emotional Organization and Disorganization

Whenever you consider emotional development, you imply a process that persists in time. Development may take place during minutes, days, years, or a lifetime. It may be rapid or gradual. Development always implies a change as well as a degree of stability.

What is emotional development? The answer depends upon how you define emotion. Unfortunately, psychologists do not at present agree upon the correct definition of emotion. See Hillman (1961).

In considering how emotion should be defined it is important to distinguish between: (1) the acute affective upset that is a contemporary event, such as fright or rage or laughter, and (2) the gradually changing disposition, or state, which develops through time. The contemporary event of emotion influences the disposition that persists and changes during the life cycle. Thus fright, with threat of impending danger, can leave a persisting state of anxiety. An insult can leave a persisting state of hostility with recurring feelings of anger and resentment. A love affair can develop a stable attitude of unselfish concern for the loved one. An emotion of disgust can leave a permanent disposition of repugnance, and so on.

I have defined emotion as an acute affective disturbance of psychological origin and extended this definition to include relatively stable, persisting states of disturbance such as anxiety or hostility or romantic love. An affective disturbance, whether acute or persisting, implies a lack of complete integration within the person.

Some psychologists have objected to defining emotion as a disturbance—a term which implies a lack of organization. For example, Leeper (1948) published a paper entitled, "A Motivational Theory of Emotion to replace 'Emotion as Disorganized Response.'" Leeper regards emotions as motivating in the sense that they initiate purposive, goal-oriented actions. He emphasizes the cognitive origin and base of emotions and their integrative role. I defended the view that emotion is a disturbance that implies an element of disorganization (Young, 1949).

Others have agreed with Leeper that emotions are integrative, not disruptive factors in the development of personality. Arnold (1960) regards emotion as an organized and felt tendency to approach or withdraw. She thoroughly considers the facts of disorganization and disruption but regards disorganization as of secondary importance. Arnold also agrees with Leeper in emphasizing the cognitive, estimative origin of emotions.

Now the truth is that affective arousals do organize attitudes, interests and aversions, motives, traits of personality, and similar dispositions. Pleasantness reinforces reactions of approach and determinations to preserve and repeat the stimulations that produce positive reactions. Unpleasantness reinforces reactions of withdrawal and avoidance of conditions that elicit negative responses.

So long as acute and chronic affective disturbances occur in nature, the concept of emotion as a disturbance is necessary and useful. Emotional disturbances are contrasted with calm, composed, affective processes and states.

GENERAL SUMMARY

Emotional development begins with the instinctive reactions that were acquired through millions of years of biological evolution. The first sign of emotion in a newborn infant is an increase in the level of general excitement or activation produced by internal and external stimulations. The cry, a mark of distress, and the smile and laugh, marks of delight, appear in the infant shortly after birth. These innate neutral, negative, and positive reactions persist through life.

Specific forms of emotional behavior such as anger, fear, and love develop gradually during the early years. They are recognized as reactions to environmental situations. At puberty with a transition to sexual maturity there are marked changes in emotional behavior and in conscious feelings, emotions, and attitudes.

Emotional maturity is achieved gradually as the child grows and gains knowledge and skill in coping with problems that arise in his environment. The outward signs of emotional disturbance may be voluntarily suppressed or openly expressed, but an adult is never completely free from feelings and emotions.

6 The Causes
of Feelings and Emotions

ATTITUDE   A manner of acting, feeling, or thinking; a disposition; a mental set. Attitudes are typically polarized (pro–con) and usually based on previous positive and negative affective arousal.

CONFLICT   The incompatibility of differing impulses; a collision of opposing ways of responding.

DISSOCIATION   A functional splitting or disintegration within the personality.

HABIT   A way of responding that has been developed through exercise, practice, training.

LATENT DISPOSITION   Traces left by previous experiences; they may be dormant for a time but reactivated by some present stimulus situation that is perceived, remembered, or imagined.

NEUROSIS   A psychological disorder characterized by one or more than one defense mechanism; leads the organism to act in a disorganized or disturbed way.

PHOBIA   An irrational and persistent fear of a particular stimulus or stimulus situation.

PSYCHOSOMATIC   A physical disorder caused by an emotional rather than a physical process.

REGRESSION   A reversion to an earlier, usually infantile form of behavior.

STRESS   A persisting condition that incites unpleasant or painful emotions.

SUPPRESSION   The inhibiting of impulses that are not desired.

Subjective feelings of comfort and discomfort depend upon the physiological state. When you are in good health and well nourished, there is a *joie de vivre,* a buoyant enjoyment of life. Foods not only taste good but they leave a deep-seated organic comfort. Muscular activity is pleasing or, at least, not unpleasant. The world has a benign appearance. Your mood is cheerful, happy. You may feel sexy. You have a positive outlook on life.

When homeostasis is disturbed, there are feelings of discomfort. We speak of *feeling* hunger, thirst, fatigue, drowsiness, eliminative pressures, and the like. We *feel* cold or hot depending on the external temperature and the state of our health. During illness we *feel* various pains, aches, pressures.

All these organically based experiences are called *feelings,* not emotions. Emotions typically have a wider field of origin than the physiological state. In emotion, as we have seen, there is always an environmental factor (present, past, or fancied) in the causation. Emotions arise from perception and/or memory of a psychological situation, including both intraorganic and environmental factors.

Emotional disturbances arise from intense stimulations, from frustrations and conflict, from stress, deprivation, and pain, as well as from the satisfaction and relief of these distressing conditions.

To understand the dynamic basis—the causes—of emotion you must take a developmental and temporal view of the inducing conditions. Emotion, as you experience it and observe it in others, is an acute affective upset. But when you speak of an emotionally disturbed person, you imply a degree of stability and permanence that develops, through time, in the underlying conditions that produce emotional expressions.

The concepts of feeling and emotion must be extended to take account of underlying dynamic conditions which have a degree of permanence.

Previous Experience as a Determinant of Feelings and Emotions

Feelings and emotions leave their imprint upon the mind. For example, consider underlying fears of specific objects or situations. Some persons show intense fear of enclosed spaces, open spaces, high places, running water, insects, and the like. These phobias are based upon a previous fright which the subject may or may not be able to recall. The fright is often complicated by a feeling of guilt. Through aided recall a phobia can sometimes be reduced or removed; but phobias tend to persist even though the subject is clearly aware of their origin.

Phobias have been given high-sounding names which add an air of profundity to the discussion but explain nothing: *pyrophobia* (fear of fire), *doraphobia* (fear of fur), *thanatophobia* (fear of death), *claustrophobia* (fear of enclosed places), *odontophobia* (fear of teeth), etc. A phobia is a latent (underlying) tendency to intense fear which is manifested in a specific stimulus situation.

We all have normal fears of situations which are threatening or dangerous. Such fears are based on previous experience. They appear to be reasonable because the dangers are real. A phobia, however, appears to most people to be irrational and its manifestation abnormally intense.

As a boy, it was my duty to turn out the lights and raise the window just before getting into bed for the night. One night, after the lights had been turned off, I was lifting the window when a gun fired with a loud BANG just below the window. A neighbor called out, "What happened? There he goes!" I could hear someone running. The experience was so terrifying that for years after the event, the raising of that particular window in the dark brought back the fear. I would not admit this to my brothers who slept in the same room, but concealed the fear. Only moving to another house solved the problem by removing the conditions that produced the fear.

What is true of fear is true also of other feelings and emotions. If an acquaintance has made an insulting remark, you are angered and retain a hostile, negative attitude of resentment. The anger leaves an imprint on the mind. The previous insult influences your present feeling as well as your behavior in the presence of the acquaintance.

And positive experiences of joy, laughter, love, and the like make impressions upon the mind that are well remembered. Previous love affairs are not forgotten. The memories may be suppressed, but emotions of the past influence present feelings.

In everyday life your latent dispositions—the ways you have learned to react to things—are aroused by perceptions—by what you see, hear, what people say, what you read, etc. Through associative memory you recall the past. And recall tends to *reinstate* the original affective quality.

The Ways We React: Latent Dispositions

There are basic scientific problems, of course, concerning the physical basis of memory and the nature of unconscious mental patterns (engrams). These problems are important and complicated; they can well be left to experts. For the layman it is sufficient to note that previous experiences leave dispositions or traces which may be latent—not appear—for indefinite periods of time and then be reactivated, revitalized by some present stimulus situation that is perceived or remembered or imagined.

There are different kinds of latent dispositions. Consider the following:

Motor habits have been developed through exercise, practice, training. They can be latent indefinitely and utilized in various motivating situations. For example, in the elementary schools you learned many verbal habits which are now latent. Suppose there is a problem. Someone asks you: How much is 9 times 6? You reply: 54. The problem activated a bit of structural organization that was latent in your nervous system. The answer popped automatically into your mind. Again, it is said that the ability to ride a bicycle is never forgotten.

Attitudes differ from habits in that they are typically polarized and usually based upon previous positive and negative affective arousals. Attitudes also differ from motives. Suppose someone asks you: Do you *like* coffee? You respond: Yes, I like coffee very much. Then there is the question: Do you *want* a cup of coffee? You say: No, thank you; I have just had three cups. Being temporarily satiated, motivation is lacking but the stable attitude persists. You insist that you *like* coffee (attitude) but do not *want* any (motivation).

Then there are *emotionally loaded memory systems.* You can recall many routine events without feeling and emotion. Remembering going to work on last April Fool's Day may arouse no particularly positive or negative feelings or emotions. This is a hedonically neutral memory. But suppose you recall the details of a love affair that ended in failure; or a stupid and embarrassing remark you made to a rival; or a fatal accident you witnessed; or the death of a loved one. Such memories, when vivid, are emotionally loaded. They revive feelings and emotions.

Finally, there are *persisting conflicts,* unsolved problems, anxiety tensions, expectations of success or failure, apprehensions, fears, hopes, and the like. All such mental dispositions persist. They are activated, or aroused, from time to time, and they can elicit intense emotional reactions. We sometimes say, "Let sleeping dogs lie!" But most people have experienced waking late at night from time to time and uncomfortably rehearsing a speech, or imagining terrible accidents befalling loved ones, or worrying about a coming exam.

Intrinsic and Extrinsic Motivation

Latent habit organization is *utilized* in goal-oriented activity. For example, consider a man rising in the morning and going to his office. He performs many habitual acts: buttoning up a shirt, eating with a knife and fork, driving a car, walking over a familiar path, unlocking and opening a door, etc. These habitual acts may be utilized in innumerable purposive activities.

In this kind of situation we say that motivation is *extrinsic* to the acts performed. By way of contrast, consider activities that are *intrinsically* motivated—activities that subjectively are pleasant, enjoyable, go along smoothly without any outside pressure. For example, eating candy does not need outside encouragement; but tasting bitter medicine is innately aversive. Most forms of play are pleasing. A healthy child plays without being taught; but extrinsic motivation may be required if he is asked to do the dishes. Adult interests are typically pleasing, carried on for their own sake; but aversions are negative and extrinsic motivation may be required.

Johnnie may enjoy his school work, but when he becomes bored with the arithmetic lesson he needs some external incentive. The teacher may motivate Johnnie by offering a prize for good work or placing a gold star beside his name or praising him or giving him a jellybean, etc. The extrinsic motivation compensates for lack of adequate intrinsic motivation.

The techniques for arousing intrinsic motivation are important for the advertiser, the propagandist, the political speaker, the evangelist, the salesman, and others who desire to control human action.

In a readable book entitled *Motivation in Advertising*, Pierre Martineau (1957), Research Director of the *Chicago Tribune*, argues on the basis of his vast experience in advertising that feeling is much more effective than argument in making people buy. People are not wholly rational. The *reason-why* type of advertisement is less effective than one that arouses feeling. Feeling is more evocative of action than logic. Being told that a motorcycle will save him transportation money motivates far fewer young men than being told of the "good life" that becomes possible for those who buy shiny new Yamahas.

Martineau illustrates his thesis with many examples. For instance, in successful advertisements of Coca-Cola, there may be a picture of happy, healthy people at the beach or in a mountain resort or at a lively party. There may be a few words like *delicious* and *refreshing*, but that is all. A person looking at the picture puts himself empathically into the situation and gets a comfortable, relaxed feeling. The positive feeling tone is associated with the product and that is enough to bias the viewer favorably toward Coca-Cola.

When you have been "sold" on a course of action you are committed. You are resolved, determined, motivated in some way. Your intrinsic motivation regulates and directs the course of your activity and utilizes whatever habit organization is available and required.

WHAT CAUSES FEELINGS AND EMOTIONS?

Rapaport (1950) wrote that a good deal of confusion concerning the definition of emotion has been due to failure of investigators to distinguish between the phenomena of emotion and the underlying dynamic mechanisms. The phenomena of emotion are complex but can be observed and analyzed from several points of view. In particular, the phenomena include: (1) the consciously experienced emotions and feelings; (2) the emotional behavior observed in man and animal; and (3) the physiological processes, especially neural and chemical, that occur during emotional disturbances.

The phenomena of emotion are observed as contemporary events. The underlying dynamic mechanisms are inferred or postulated, regardless of the observer's point of view. Among the dynamic conditions that elicit feelings and emotions are the following:

Intense Stimulations

For every task that you carry out there is an optimal degree of motivation. This is shown schematically in Figure 13. The figure illustrates what is commonly meant by undermotivation, optimal motivation, and overmotivation. If you think of motivation in terms of activation through sensory stimulation, then the base line represents different intensities of stimulation. The illustration implies that motivation is a quantitative variable and that the level of performance varies with the intensity of stimulation.

To illustrate: Suppose a man, in a laboratory test, is given the arbitrary task of sorting and packing spools of different sizes. If he makes an error, a weak electric shock is given to the arm. This weak incentive increases both the accuracy and speed of performance. But if an intense shock is administered, the subject makes random and excessive movements with arms and legs, frowns, cries out in pain,

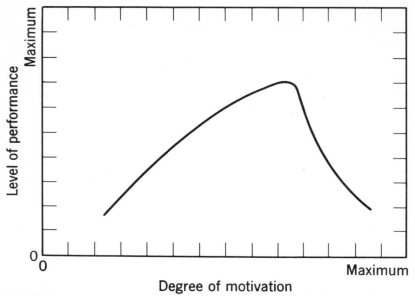

Figure 13. Representation of the general relation between level of performance and degree of motivation.

attempts to escape from the situation. His performance is disrupted. With intense painful stimulation a man is said to "lose his head," "go to pieces," "become emotionally disturbed," "be disorganized."

Many experiments have been made with both laboratory animals and human subjects to test what is known as the Yerkes-Dodson law. According to this law there is an optimal level of incentive for every experimental task. If the level of incentive is above the optimum, performance is impaired and may become emotionally disrupted.

The Yerkes-Dodson law relates the optimal incentive to the difficulty of the task. For example, if animals are given the task of discriminating visual brightnesses, the difficulty of the task can be increased by presenting brightnesses that are increasingly similar. An easy task would be discriminating black from white. The Yerkes-Dodson law states that *as the difficulty of a task increases, the strength of shock that yields optimal performance approaches the threshold value.* This means that a *weaker* shock is required to give optimal performance on a difficult task than on an easy one.

If this principle turns out to have general validity (and there are indications that it does), there are practical implications. For example, if a bright boy and a dull boy are working on some problem in arithmetic, the problem will be easier for the bright boy. If optimal performance is desired from both boys, the dull boy should have weaker "punishment" (or possibly stronger "rewards") than the bright child.

Much of the laboratory work concerning stimulation intensity has been done with electric shocks and nonhuman subjects. It is known, however, that weak electric shocks are hedonically neutral or even positive (interesting) as incentives to human beings. Moderate and strong shocks are negative; subjects are aversive to them. Intense shocks are emotionally disruptive and disorganizing. A shock has three effects varying with intensity: it can be instructive, have incentive value, or be disruptive.

Apart from painful stimulations, however, many other sensory excitations elicit pleasant or neutral feelings at low intensities but at high intensities they become disagreeable. Dazzling and flickering lights, shrill and high-pitched tones, pungent odors, astringent and bitter tastes, as well as painful stimulations, are unpleasant. The normal reaction to such intense stimulations is aversive.

Ulrich, Hutchinson, and Azrin (1965) have shown that painful stimulations tend to elicit fighting and aggressive attack in many animals, including man. Hence aggression is one effect of intense painful stimulation. Aggressive fighting is commonly regarded as a basic form of emotional behavior. If you accidentally cut yourself, you are annoyed but if someone intentionally hurts you, you are angered and prone to fight back.

Frustration and Interruption of Behavior

It is the thesis of Dollard et al. (1939) that whenever aggressive behavior appears, it shows that the aggressor has been frustrated in some way; in other words, aggressive behavior is caused by frustration. The converse of this proposition, however, is not necessarily true, for frustration can lead to emotional upsets without aggression. It can also lead to regression—a return to an earlier and less adaptive mode of reacting. There are instances in which resignation and passive acceptance are the response to a frustrating situation. Frustration commonly results in weeping and other forms of emotional reaction without aggression. But by and large, the most frequent reaction to frustration is retaliative and aggressive behavior. (See page 77.)

The most direct form of aggressive behavior is physical attack upon the frustrating object to destroy, injure, remove it, or to change the frustrating situation. If direct attack is impossible, displaced aggression may appear. Thus a man, frustrated by his boss in the office, puts on a smile and says nothing, but when he comes home at night he may threaten the dog, spank his child, or complain about supper. The blame and hostility can readily be shifted from one victim to another.

At a meeting of the American Psychological Association, an English psychologist told this story of a man who was hurrying to catch a London subway train already standing in the station. He started to put a coin in the glass coin-box beside the gate. Then he noticed that the coin (still in his fingers) was a half-crown instead of a penny. He was in a dilemma that demanded immediate decision. He could drop the coin and catch the train or he could rescue the coin and risk missing the train. He took the latter course. Slowly and with difficulty he raised the coin from the coin-box, holding it tightly. Then the coin, nearly extricated, slipped between his fingers and fell back into the box just as the train left. He had lost both the coin and the train! Doubly frustrated, he walked down the platform. A short distance away was a man (a complete stranger), with one foot on a bench, tying his shoe. Impulsively and without pausing he gave the man a boot on the seat of the pants, saying, "Damn it, you are always tying your shoe!"

Mandler (1964) prefers to speak of the *interruption* of behavior, rather than frustration, as a principal cause of emotional behavior. When a behavioral sequence is interrupted, a person tends to want to complete the activity in progress. Other reactions that cannot be integrated with the ongoing, planned behavior are disorganizing and emotional. For example, a man riding a bicycle is hurrying to an important engagement. He passes a friend and waves a hearty greeting. Waving does not interfere with bicycle riding and there is no emotion. Suppose, however, that the friend stopped the rider and engaged him in a lengthy conversation. The cyclist, concerned over reaching his destination on time, would be thrown into conflict and become emotionally disturbed by the delay. It is the *interruption* of planned, purposive behavior that produces the emotion.

Conflict

John Dewey, the philosopher, described a conflict theory of emotion which was then reformulated in simpler terms by Angier (1927). Dewey used the above example of a bicycle rider to show how conflict causes emotion. "*Without* a conflict, there is no emotion; *with* it, there is," Dewey said. He saw emotion as a conflict state. The conflict theory of emotion has limitations, for there are obviously other causes of emotion than conflict. Also, there are nonemotional conflicts and decisions.

But persisting unresolved conflicts are an important cause of emotional outbreaks. Consider, for example, the case of a young man who has fallen in love. He would like to marry the girl, but he has a hereditary physical defect which he does not wish to transmit to the oncoming generation. He believes that the girl, being healthy and of a maternal nature, is entitled to have a child of her own. Thus he is in deep conflict about marrying. Finally he "pops the question," but the girl turns him down. This makes him keenly aware of his physical inferiority and accentuates the conflict. His work suffers. The conflict involves basic biological and social motivations. The conflict state itself is psychological.

There are several considerations regarding conflict. The emotional state is much more than frustration or interruption of a single plan or motive. Self-regarding feelings and anxiety are also involved. Our young man may develop such a feeling of low self-worth and anxiety about himself that he begins to drink heavily, and avoids social contacts with women.

Luria (1932) performed a series of famous studies of human conflicts from the standpoint of disorganization of motor, including verbal, behavior. In one of the studies his subjects were students about to take a critical examination. In the spring of 1924, during the Russian revolution, the government decided to drastically cut down the student enrollment. Every student had to appear before a commission that considered his academic activity. If the commission decided unfavorably, the candidate was expelled from the school, destroying his plans for future education. If the decision was favorable, he could continue his academic career. This was no ordinary examination, since everything depended on its outcome. It was called a "purge" or "cleansing."

Luria removed students from a waiting line just a few minutes before this important examination. He then recorded voluntary and involuntary muscular movements and verbal responses to particular words. Some of the stimulus words presented for free association were neutral: *day, pillow, gold.* Others referred to the traumatic situation: *examination, cleansing, commission.* At the instant the subject responded verbally he squeezed a bulb with the right hand and also attempted to hold a weight steady with the left. Graphic records were obtained of the pattern of voluntary contraction and of involuntary steadiness. There was clear evidence that the pattern of motor control was disturbed.

There was also blocking or obstruction of the associative processes. The verbal reaction times to indifferent words were lengthened if these words came in a period shortly after the critical words.

Luria described the gross behavior of a typical subject as follows: "Very excited, talking loudly, fidgeting in his chair, striking his hands on the table, continuously conversing, conversing in spite of being asked to keep quiet, scolding. He responds to the stimulus in fluctuating tones, sometimes in an ordinary voice and again very boisterously. Further investigations reveal a marked variability in the strength of motor pressures; sometimes he strikes the dynamo-scope. Toward the end of the experiment he says he cannot continue the experiment as he must wait his turn in line."

Luria pointed out that such emotional disorganization is not a transient process. There is a chronic anxiety that outlasts the manifest emotion and that can be understood only in the light of the stressful situation. In other words, to understand emotional disturbances you must go beyond the acute, temporary manifestations to the basic underlying dynamic processes.

The Release of Tension

The conditions of intense and painful stimulation, frustration and interruption, or conflict tend to build up unpleasant excited feelings and a persisting state of tension and stress. Feelings and emotions also arise from conditions that release tension. Weeping and laughing, joy and sorrow, and ecstasy are all caused by the release of tension that has been built up. The removal of stress and tension brings an affective reaction.

We have seen in earlier chapters how cerebral control is weakened during emotional disturbances so that subcerebral centers (thalamus, hypothalamus, limbic system, and autonomic nervous system) take over partial control. Under conditions of extreme conflict and anxiety, physiological responses become disorganized and we can describe the person as being emotionally upset. Picture a waitress who is feeling guilty that she is at work because her seven-year-old son is pitching a Little League game. Yet she knows that if she asks for a day off she may lose her job, which she needs desperately. A busload of hot and impatient travelers arrives, the coffee machine breaks down, everyone is in a hurry to be served, and the boss is watching her. At this moment she feels her bra strap break and then her activities become almost a slapstick drama of indecisive, disorganized activity. In this condition, being a rather healthy and cheerful person, she sits down and has a good laugh, releasing the tension and preparing herself for renewed attack upon the many physiological, mental, emotional traumas at hand.

Why do we weep? Lund (1930) found that weeping occurs in complex, typically social situations. It is not merely a great loss or bereavement which brings tears. Lund's investigation showed that it is often the presence of some alleviating or redeeming feature in an otherwise distressing situation that is the immediate occasion for tears. (In the case of our waitress, the broken strap provided a humorous relief. She might have responded by hysterical weeping.) At a funeral the tears flow when the speaker eulogizes the deceased by saying that he was a wonderful father, a great-hearted citizen, a loving husband, well loved in the community, etc. It is the emphasis upon the goodness and personal value of the lost loved one that brings tears. This emphasis accentuates a conflict between the reality of death and the value of the deceased. Weeping is the emotional release from the aroused conflict. Incidentally, Lund found, contrary to common belief, that a deep depressive psychosis is tearless. The pathological depression has a biochemical basis which is not relieved by transient events and tears.

Why do we laugh? Philosophers, psychologists, novelists, and others have attempted to answer this question but there is little agreement. Hayworth (1928) argued that laughter has a social origin and function; it develops as a form of communication. In a tense situation in which there is impending danger or strain, laughter is the signal that all is well. Through a smile or laughter one flashes the meaning, "Have no fear; I will not hurt you; all is well."

Hayworth summarized the conditions which are said to elicit laughter: (1) *triumph or victory,* whether in battle or in a game of cards, brings a feeling of personal superiority and laughter. (2) *Surprise* of a kind which brings a feeling of superiority. The practical joke, an easy victory, or an unexpected reward may bring joy, smiling and laughter. (3) *Tickling,* especially in children, appears to induce a sort of reflexive laughter. The tickler assumes the role of attacker and then stimulates in a light playful way, thus releasing tension. (4) *Incongruous situations—* incongruity covers a considerable range of humor. Recall the famous situation in which a dignified man slips on a banana peel. (5) A *sense of well-being, sound health, security in social situations* is also associated with laughter. The healthy child laughs spontaneously, naturally, and with slight provocation. (6) Finally, there is the *voluntary, nervous* laugh. A person may laugh to appear cheerful in a social situation. Consider the practical joker, the back-slapping "life of the party." He may actually be a lonely person whose actions reflect an overwhelming need to appear part of every social situation. His constant tricks and loud laughter are enacted voluntarily, and do not constitute a reflexive expression of real joy.

In general, both weeping and laughing occur with release of tension. The result may be pleasant or unpleasant. For example, consider a parent watching a child with pneumonia or some other critical illness. If the crisis is passed successfully, there may be tearful relief expressing joy; if the child dies, there is sorrowful weeping and grief. The release of tension brings the emotion.

Suppressed Motivations

We are constantly on guard against the use of four-letter words that refer to eliminative and sexual functions. In polite society these words are taboo. According to Freud's theory of wit and humor, there is an internal censorship that blocks the utterance of such words. The smutty story told in appropriate circumstances avoids the censorship, in some way, and produces laughter. And everyone knows someone who always seems to be able to get away with shady jokes. Some persons are less inhibited; others are overcontrolled and careful to do and say the "right" thing. There is a healthy middle ground.

Even though we are aware of taboo words, we tend to avoid utterance of them. McGinnies (1949) coined the phrase "perceptual defense" to designate the resistance we have against the recognition of words that are socially taboo. This resistance was demonstrated by tachistoscopic exposures of words with exposure times too brief to permit complete recognition. The threshold times for recognition were determined by exposing stimulus words for 0.1 second, 0.2 second, etc. until complete recognition and verbal report occurred. McGinnies determined the threshold recognition times for each of sixteen subjects, eight males and eight females.

In the main experiment, eighteen words were presented one at a time. Eleven of these words were neutral and seven of them were critical, i.e., taboo words. The list follows with critical words in italics:

1. Apple	7. River	13. *Penis*
2. Dance	8. *Whore*	14. Music
3. *Raped*	9. Sleep	15. Trade
4. Child	10. *Kotex*	16. *Filth*
5. *Belly*	11. Broom	17. Clear
6. Glass	12. Stove	18. *Bitch*

The subjects were told that they would be shown some words which they might not be able to recognize at first. They were instructed to report whatever they saw or thought they saw on each exposure, regardless of what it was. They were asked to delay their report until a signal was given by the experimenter. The purpose of the delay was to allow about 6 seconds for the appearance and recording of the galvanic skin response (GSR)—an index of involuntary action of the autonomic nervous system. Before the experiment, electrodes were strapped to the palms of the hands for recording the GSR.

Average data for the group are presented in Figure 14. This figure shows the mean threshold times (in seconds) required for the recognition of neutral and critical words. The chart shows that the times are consistently longer for the recognition of critical (taboo) words than for the neutral (non-taboo) words. The average difference between neutral and critical words is statistically significant.

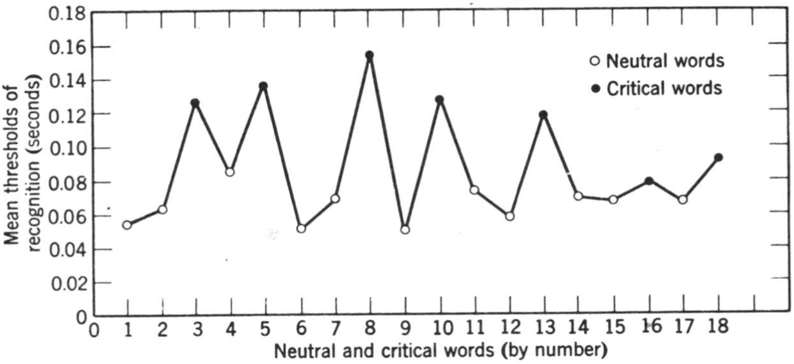

Figure 14. Mean thresholds of recognition, in seconds, for neutral and critical words. Redrawn from McGinnies (1949).

The data for the GSR showed a heightened autonomic response on *prerecognition* times for the critical words. It is interesting that there is an affective reaction *before* the stimulus words are clearly recognized, as well as an increase in recognition time.

McGinnies calls this resistance to recognizing of taboo words "perceptual defense." He believes that the defense is a way of avoiding anxiety created by briefly exposed taboo words. Early in life the child is taught that certain words are naughty and must not be used. A child may be familiar with the bad words, but if he uses them, he is punished. Thus there is built up a resistance to the use and recognition of obscene words in polite society.

Suppressed motivations are commonly found in persons accused of criminal or immoral acts. If a man has knowledge of guilt which he wishes to conceal, he may be emotionally disturbed and blush when questioned about his criminal or immoral act. A guilty person might be able to control facial expressions and tell lies voluntarily with little outward sign of emotion. He may "play it cool," but in most cases vascular and other involuntary changes occur and can be recorded.

The lie detector is an instrument for recording *involuntary* changes in pulse and blood pressure, respiration, and the GSR. When we say that these changes are *involuntary* we mean that they cannot be suppressed by the subject.

The lie detector is really an emotion detector. The difference between truth and falsehood is not a *psychological* difference but rather one related to logic and morals. What the lie detector really detects is the presence or absence of an emotional disturbance. If a person *feels* embarrassed or ashamed or guilty while making a false or even a true statement, the involuntary changes in pulse, blood pressure, respiration, and GSR will occur. But there are people who can make false statements with complete composure. In such cases, the lie detector will record no emotional disturbance. Use of this instrument requires great skill and knowledge.

Unconscious Motivations

Freud, as we know, emphasized unconscious motivation. He taught that slips of the tongue, forgetting appointments, losing objects, breaking things seemingly by accident, awkward movements, and other phenomena of everyday life are motivated by determinants of which the subject is not consciously aware. Even dreams, daydreams, and flights of fantasy are caused by unconscious motivations. All behavior, according to Freud, is motivated. It is the task of psychoanalysis to discover and reveal to the conscious subject his unconscious motivations and to help him cope with them.

You may voluntarily *suppress,* or inhibit, impulses that you regard as unworthy and want to forget. Thus you may inhibit the impulse to tell a dirty story or to use taboo words. You may refuse to think about a cutting remark made by a friend.

Repression is different from simple suppression or inhibition. Repression is a process that places experiences beyond the awareness of the individual so that he cannot voluntarily recall them. Feelings of anxiety or guilt or impulses of hostility and sex may become repressed. The individual becomes unconscious of the basic motivations and emotional conflicts. He may exhibit bizarre symptoms, however, as long as the unconscious motivation and conflict are present.

Repression implies *dissociation*—a functional splitting or disintegration within the personality. A person who is dissociated may not respond to sights and sounds of his or her environment, being apparently absorbed in an inner mental life. According to Cameron and Magaret (1951), the conditions that lead to repression and dissociation are these: (1) an unsolved personal conflict in which something of great importance is at stake; (2) anxiety based on the anticipation of misfortune or punishment; (3) a threat to one's self-esteem or prestige—i.e., an ego factor.

Janet's classical case of dissociation (technically known as a somnambulism because it resembles ordinary sleep-walking) has been described in Bernard Hart's (1937), *The Psychology of Insanity*:

> A French girl, Irène, had nursed her mother through a long illness that culminated in death. The trying experiences and painful events produced a profound shock upon the patient's mind. Then a somnambulism developed. Irène, engaged in sewing or conversation at the moment, would suddenly cease her occupation and commence to live over again the painful scenes of her mother's death, enacting each detail with the power of an accomplished actress. While the drama was in progress she appeared to hear nothing that was said to her and to be oblivious of her environment. She was living in a world of fantasy. Quite suddenly Irène, seemingly unaware of the fact that anything unusual had happened, would return to her former occupation. After an interval of perhaps several days another somnambulism, similar in most respects to the previous ones, would abruptly appear and vanish. During the apparently

normal periods between somnambulisms the patient was unaware of what had occurred and, moreover, unable to recall the system of ideas and feelings connected with her mother's death. She remembered nothing of the illness nor of its tragic end. She discussed her mother's death without feeling and was reproached by relatives for her callous indifference.

In this classical case of repression and dissociation there was an emotional situation—an intensely unpleasant experience associated with the mother's illness and death. Irène had been personally involved in the tragedy. The entire system of memories and feelings became dissociated from the main stream of consciousness.

When functional dissociation is complete there is splitting off of a system of experiences so that one mental system does not have memory access to the other. The repressed system asserts itself from time to time, as in cases of dual or multiple personality, but between eruptions the dissociated complex remains unconscious. Dissociation and repression are nature's crude way of solving an emotional conflict and freeing the individual from an intolerable situation.

EMOTION AND MENTAL HEALTH

Dr. George M. Beard, in 1876, read a paper before the American Neurological Association in New York entitled, "The Influence of Mind in the Causation and Cure of Disease and the Potency of Definite Expectations." Dr. Beard maintained that disease might appear and disappear without influence of any other agent than some form of emotion. He regarded fear, terror, anxiety, grief, anger, wonder, or a definite expectation as mental conditions likely to produce disease. Dr. Beard argued that certain emotional states could neutralize the therapeutics and increase the effects of drugs. At the time, his ideas were new and startling. Today these ideas are recognized in a movement known as psychosomatic medicine.

It is widely accepted now that persisting emotional disturbances constitute an important factor in certain disorders: peptic ulcers, essential hypertension, rheumatoid arthritis, ulcerative colitis, bronchial asthma, hyperthyroidism, neurodermatitis, and other disorders. The health of the patient is strongly influenced by conditions of living which produce emotional traumata, such as financial failure, bereavement, insult, injury, unrequited love, threatened divorce, loss of self-esteem, feelings of guilt, chronic physical disease, and other factors of tension and stress. Today psychogenic disorders are well recognized by the medical and psychological professions.

The Medical View of Stress

The conditions that incite unpleasant emotions—painful stimulation, frustration and interruption, conflict, insult, etc.—are also factors that produce stress. But stress is a broader, more comprehensive concept than emotion. Persisting cold, hunger, fatigue, loss of sleep, disease, danger and threat, and other conditions produce tension and stress. These same conditions, when persistent, *predispose* the individual toward repeated emotional outbreaks but do not necessarily *elicit* emotional reactions. Under stress, however, there may develop a neurosis or even a nervous breakdown.

Hans Selye, as a young medical student, was impressed by the fact that most diseases are accompanied by nonspecific symptoms, such as fever. A specific disease has a specific syndrome, but there is also a nonspecific syndrome that simply indicates that the individual is sick. The nonspecific syndrome can be studied independently and apart from any specific disorder.

When some factor of stress is present, the body reacts to it with a *general adaptation syndrome.* Writes Selye (1956):

> I call this syndrome *general,* because it is produced only by agents which have a general effect upon large portions of the body. I call it *adaptive* because it stimulates defense and thereby helps the acquisition and maintenance of the stage of inurement. I call it a *syndrome* because its individual manifestations are coordinated even partly dependent upon each other.

The general adaptation syndrome manifests itself in three ways: (1) there is enlargement of the adrenal cortex; (2) there is shrinkage of the thymus, the spleen, the lymph nodes, and all other lymphatic structures in the body; (3) there is bleeding, and deep *ulcers* form in the lining of the stomach and uppermost part of the gut. There are further symptoms of the reaction to stress such as loss of body weight, alterations in the chemical composition of the body, etc.

The general adaptive reaction to stress is a physiological unit involving the pituitary gland, the adrenals, the thymus glands, the stomach, and the white blood corpuscles. These structures provide a unitary defense of the body against the diverse forms of damage from stress factors.

According to Selye, stress is a fundamental medical and biological concept with broad practical and philosophical implications. Stress is closely related to the maintaining of homeostasis and to resistance of the body against disease; but stress cannot be identified with disturbed homeostasis nor with the power of the body to fight disease. Injury to the tissues, infections from the attacks of bacteria, fatigue, hunger, thirst, pain, and similar conditions, as well as frustrations, anxiety, and threats, are factors that tend to produce or augment stress.

Selye believes that each individual has a certain quantity of *adaptation energy.* This is not the same as caloric energy (usually considered to be the fuel of life) because exhaustion can occur even when ample food is available. He believes that "every living being has a certain innate amount of *adaptation energy* or vitality. This can be used slowly for a long and uneventful life, or rapidly during a shorter and more stressful, but often also, more colorful and enjoyable existence." We are reminded of burning the candle at both ends!

Selye states three lessons derived from research on stress: first, our body can meet the most diverse aggressions with the same adaptive defensive mechanism. Second, this mechanism can be identified and its parts described in measurable physical and chemical terms, such as changes in the structure of organs that produce hormones. Third, we need information about stress to lay the foundations for a new kind of treatment, the essence of which is to combat disease by strengthening the body's own defenses against stress.

Stress and Neurosis

In times of war and other crises, men are called upon to endure hardship for long periods of time. A man may suffer from fatigue or exhaustion, hunger, loss of sleep, and pain and also suffer persistent anxiety concerning the safety and security of others. Such factors accumulate, producing acute stress and emotional tension.

During World War II two psychiatrists, Doctors Grinker and Spiegel (1945), examined combat aviators who were called upon to fly in repeated bombing missions. Their book, *Men under Stress,* gives a clear account of the stress that develops under war conditions.

The unending strain eventually produces distress signals. Enthusiasm and eagerness give way to a weariness of battle, which is then endured because there is no way out. Transient fears turn into permanent apprehensions. Anxiety has a tendency to spread until it is continuous or is aroused by trivial sounds. Good muscular coordination is replaced by uncontrollable tremors, jerky manipulations, and tensions. Constant tension leads to restlessness that is intolerant of repose and never satisfied by activity. Sleep dwindles and gives way altogether to insomnia punctured by fitful nightmares. Appetite is reduced and gastric difficulties appear. Although air sickness is rare, nausea and vomiting after meals, especially breakfast, are fairly common, as is a functional diarrhea. Frequency of urination, headache, and backache are common signs of the body's reaction to emotional stress. With the growing lack of control over mental and physical reactions comes a grouchiness and irritability that interferes with good relations among the men. Some give way easily, and are always in a quarrel or argument. Others become depressed and seclusive, and stay away from their friends to avoid dissension, or because they feel ashamed. Thinking and behavior may become seriously altered. Forgetfulness, preoccupation, constant brooding over the loss of friends, and combat experiences, impair purposeful activity. The behavior of the men becomes not only asocial but completely inappropriate and bizarre.

To avoid stigmatizing the flier, these reactions are roughly grouped under the undiagnostic term of "operational fatigue." The symptoms do not fall into clear-cut diagnostic categories.

There are many current situations that produce stress, for example, a person undergoing the strain of a long divorce or a woman whose husband in Vietnam is missing in action.

Frustration Tolerance and Nervous Breakdown

Individuals differ widely in their ability to tolerate stress and frustration. Some persons fly into a towering rage at the slightest provocation. Others respond to a frustrating situation in a matter-of-fact way; they are the more stable emotionally. But there is a limit to the amount of frustration and emotional stress that an individual can tolerate.

Guthrie (1938), writing of nervous breakdowns, has put it this way:

Probably any man could be placed in a situation which would bring on such collapse. Some situations are intolerable for any human beings. Central American prisons in the old days, solitary confinement in verminous dungeons, torture, cumulative misfortune, can put any man in the condition which we describe as nervous breakdown. But there are great differences in what different individuals can tolerate. (231)

When painful, distressing factors are added together, the cumulative stress will sooner or later break anyone down. There is a limit to what the organism can tolerate. And there are wide individual differences in frustration tolerance. A housewife has developed a high tolerance for the noise and confusion of four active children, but her husband cannot tolerate the noise. He in turn has a higher tolerance than she for the demands for deadlines and for business requirements.

The proneness to emotional upset as well as to nervous breakdown varies with age, habituation to an environmental situation, physiological state, and many other factors. An adult can tolerate more frustration than a child, without showing emotion. The hardened soldier can tolerate, without emotional upset, more hardship than the new recruit. But fatigue, hunger, cold, loss of sleep, and similar conditions can make any individual (especially the child) more ready to respond emotionally.

NORMAL AND ABNORMAL EMOTIONAL REACTIONS

Every day we read in the paper about some bit of abnormal behavior that has psychological causation. The news is typically disturbing:

> A girl has taken LSD and, believing she can fly, jumps out of the hotel window to her death.
> A man in love with a girl shoots and kills a rival lover.
> A professor of sociology, depressed over the state of human society, shoots himself.
> A quiet, well-mannered teenager shoots his parents and his four brothers and sisters to death on Christmas Eve.
> A mother walks into the ocean, trying to drown herself and her two young children.

Such bits of human behavior occur occasionally. Most of us would regard them as abnormal. One thing is clear, however: human behavior depends upon the mental state of the agent. And the mental state includes both the cognitive and emotional aspects of subjective experience.

Psychiatry and Clinical Psychology

Psychiatry is a medical discipline. *Psychology* is a basic science that deals with mental, including behavioral, phenomena wherever and whenever they occur. The modern psychiatrist is medically trained and also well grounded in the medical aspects of psychology.

When mental illness is produced by chemicals and drugs, by brain injury, by viruses and bacteria, by emotional stress, and the like, a psychiatrist should be consulted. But there is a wide range of normal problems arising from personal difficulties in coping with the social and natural environment. In this area of normal adjustments to emotional problems the clinical psychologist and psychological counsellor can be of great service.

Mental disorders have a dual basis. One is *psychosomatic;* the other *somatopsychic.* The complete and adequate understanding of mental disorders requires both the subjective and objective views of psychological phenomena.

Psychotherapy

Psychotherapy is not merely an intellectual process. It has wrongly been said that the way to bring about readjustment is to help the patient gain an intellectual understanding of his problems. A cognitive understanding of one's life situation is helpful but not sufficient to effect a cure and solution.

Psychotherapy operates in the sphere of emotion. Its aim is to provide corrective emotional experience by relaxing the subject's defenses and permitting him to reappraise the situation that produced anxiety, hostility, or other emotional state. In the major methods of psychotherapy the subject is encouraged to *feel,* to express his feelings and emotions. Emotional expressions are of primary importance. They can, of course, be supplemented by rational suggestions, arguments, persuasions. A combination of rational and emotional approaches is necessary in psychotherapy.

Psychoanalysts have long recognized the importance of emotion in the etiology and therapy of neuroses. Unresolved conflicts, anxieties, repressed hostilities, loss of self-esteem, and similar conditions underlie neurotic symptoms. To reveal the unconscious motivations and alleviate mental disorder, psychoanalysts have resorted to free verbal association, hypnosis, aided recall, and interpretation of dreams, all the while observing emotional expressions. The clinical aim of psychotherapy is to elicit thoughts and the accompanying emotional reactions.

A dominant emotion is associated with something important to the patient, something that affects him deeply. Just why it is important can be learned only by getting the patient to talk, to express his thoughts along with his feelings and emotions.

Mental Hygiene

There is a wide range of *normal* feelings and emotions that arise during the course of everyday living. They come from the frustrations and conflicts of human existence. Emotional problems rise on every side from the interpersonal and social relations with which you are involved.

You experience feelings and emotions from which there is no escape. What are these feelings? Upon what dynamic conditions do they depend? What, if anything, can you do about them? How can you cope with the emotional problems that arise from your environmental and social situation?

In the next chapter some of these emotional problems will be considered. They are problems and situations that indicate the need for mental hygiene—the keeping of a sound mind.

GENERAL SUMMARY

Emotional upsets are hedonically *positive* in joy, laughter, ecstasy; *neutral* during routine activities and great excitement; *negative* in pain, weeping, grief.

Emotional upsets occur during certain predisposing conditions. Among these conditions are past experiences of anger, fear, love, pain, disgust, joy, sorrow, and other emotional experiences. Through past emotional experiences you develop states of anxiety, hostility, love, hate, guilt, etc. These mental states strongly predispose you to feelings and emotions. Feelings arise from the perception, memory and imagination of situations that previously aroused them. Also, persisting conditions of stress and strain such as hunger, illness, and other uncomfortable states predispose you to emotional reactions.

Among the conditions that directly cause feelings and emotions are painful stimulations, frustrations, interruptions, conflicts, persisting tension, and the release of tension. The expectation of a pleasant or unpleasant effect can also cause an emotional reaction.

Negative mental states affect your well-being, your health and happiness. Glandular and organic disorders strongly influence your life of feeling, and in extreme disorders medical help and psychological counseling may be needed to restore composure and regain a healthy outlook on life.

7 Emotion in Personal and Social Problems

ADJUSTMENT The arrival at a particular means of responding to disorganization of mental states in order to achieve stability, balance. Adjustment can be psychologically "healthy" or it can include the use of various defense reactions that do not necessarily lead the individual to a "normal" and well-balanced emotional state.

ANXIETY An enduring fear based on the anticipation or expectancy of harm. Anxiety is a conflict state.

EGO A psychological entity designated by Freud to be the agency that reconciles the claims of the *id* with reality, environmental forces, and the *superego*.

EGO-INVOLVEMENT Concern with the self as an individual distinct from other individuals and things.

EMPATHY The ability to "see" into another person's personality in order to understand him better. The vicarious experiencing of the feelings of another.

ID The blind, primitive instincts, especially those of sex and hostility that are unconscious.

IDENTIFICATION The placing of oneself in a particular context in which one feels he "belongs." Ego-involvement is a form of identification.

PSYCHOPATHIC Suffering from a mental disorder; usually associated with those disturbances in which amoral, conscience-less behavior is typical.

SUPEREGO The "voice of the parent"; conscience; the ideal self with standards of correct conduct.

To understand the feelings and emotions of human beings you must know something about their social and cultural environment. You must understand the *Weltanschauung*—the world view—of individuals living within a particular social group, and the problems, difficulties, and requirements that a social situation presents.

Feelings and emotions arise in your attempt to cope with elements in your natural and social worlds.

FEELINGS DETERMINED BY SELF-REGARDING ATTITUDES AND MOTIVES

Your relationship to other human beings plays a tremendously important role in the development of feelings and emotions. You are constantly evaluating and comparing yourself with others.

In the following sections, some of these self-regarding feelings and emotions will be considered.

Feelings and Attitudes of Inferiority

The infant perceives his bodily self in relation to his mother and others in the immediate environment. He is dependent upon others for nourishment, cleanliness, comfort, and love. He is self-centered—a little animal whose feelings are determined only by perception of his body and his immediate surroundings.

When the infant has matured into childhood, he sees and hears himself compared with others. John is bigger and stronger than you; he can knock you down and fight better. Mary can run faster. Harry can throw a ball farther. Jim lives in a finer house, has a bigger yard and better clothes than you. Lisa's dad drives a better car; your folks have only a jalopy. Joe's father owns a store, your father is a janitor. These comparisons go on and on. The discriminations are *cognitive* in nature. They tend to build up both negative attitudes and feelings of self-regard.

When I was a schoolboy, a classmate once gave me a dime. I asked why. He said because his dad had more money than my dad. I did not understand at that time why my mother made me return the dime the next day.

Of course, the comparisons may be the other way around. Perhaps you are the biggest and strongest child in your group. You can run faster, get better grades than the others. Perhaps your folks have the bigger house and better car. You have the more attractive play equipment. On the playground, in fights, in the classroom, at home, this self-*versus*-other comparison goes on endlessly, with the result that you perceive yourself as superior. Others accept your leadership. You develop feelings and attitudes of self-confidence.

Other factors being equal, it is usually size, physical attractiveness, and superior achievement in school that allows particular children to dominate others in a group and to become leaders. Success builds self-confidence. Failure negates self-confidence and brings a feeling of inferiority.

If a child has some obvious physical defect—obesity, short stature, a crippled limb, an unsightly birthmark, deafness—other children usually make him repeatedly and painfully aware of it. His cognitive awareness engenders a feeling of personal inferiority that persists indefinitely. Often the child who is defective or handicapped is repeatedly frustrated in social situations. He recognizes his inferiority and is thrown into mental conflict. He sometimes withdraws from group activities. Or he may suppress the conflict state and put on a bold front.

With adults there are positive and negative self-regarding attitudes based upon such things as wealth, social position, skin color, language, nationality, religion, physical prowess, and other factors. The perception of an inferior status builds up feelings and attitudes of inferiority and they, in turn, influence an individual's behavior.

Feelings of inferiority are commonly based on subjective, self-imposed standards of conduct. There is the inferiority-ridden person who actually is doing well but fails to live up to some self-imposed standard and therefore is miserable. Others would not blame him but he blames himself.

It often happens that a person is not aware of the dynamic factors that influence his feelings. The nature of the conflict that engenders feelings of inferiority may not enter awareness. The inferiority complex may be repressed and unconscious.

Self-regarding attitudes and motives play an important role in the development of personality. These factors make one person shy and retiring, another bold and aggressive. Self-regarding attitudes of inferiority are often at the root of persisting failures to make suitable adjustments. And they are circular—the worse a person considers himself, the more inferior he will *appear*, thus causing him to act in certain ways and fulfilling his own perception of himself as being of low worth.

Alfred Adler pointed out that persons with an inferiority complex tend to compensate in various ways for their feelings of less worth. History records well-known examples of men with defects who have compensated for the defect and achieved greatness. Demosthenes had a speech impediment; he practiced speaking (it is reported) with pebbles in his mouth and became a great orator. Lord Byron had a club foot; despite this defect he wrote immortal poetry. Steinmetz, a cripple, became a wizard of electricity. Kaiser Wilhelm, who had a withered arm, became a military leader. Beethoven, who was deaf, composed great symphonies. Jimmy Durante capitalized on his oversized nose.

Levels and Areas of Aspiration

Compensation for feelings of inferiority can be achieved by changing the level of aspiration or by shifting from one area of activity and professed competence to another.

Rotter (1942) pointed out that the goal an individual sets for himself is dependent upon two main factors. First, there is the wish to excel, to improve, to do better than other persons, to achieve competence. Second, there is a realistic estimate of one's ability based on knowledge of success and failure in previous performances. This knowledge tends to keep the level of aspiration at a realistic level.

Feelings of self-confidence and inferiority are based upon success and failure in activities that you deem to be important. You set for yourself standards of performance. You may succeed or fail relative to a self-imposed standard.

A person has ambition to succeed in certain areas of activity. He evaluates his competence in these areas. If he is confronted with failure in one area, he may shift to another. Suppose a college student who is failing in a mathematics course abandons math as a field of endeavor, deciding he is not a mathematician. He goes out for baseball. If his performance in baseball convinces him that he is only mediocre, he may turn to social life in the hope of becoming a "hail fellow well met" or just a "gentleman." Such shifts in the area of professed ambition and aspiration protect the ego from a sense of defeat and failure. A person's level of aspiration, formed by his experiences with success and failure as he matures, can have a lot to do with the kind of life he has. Some people have a level of aspiration that is deliberately set too high ("There, I *told* you I couldn't do it! See? I'm just no good!").

Shifting from one area of professed competence to another area is a form of compensation that protects the individual from feelings of inferiority. It is important that a person gain a feeling of competence, success, worthwhileness, and self-confidence in at least one area of activity.

Feelings of Self-Confidence, Pride, and Humility

Self-confidence is based on personal achievement and the way your performance is regarded by others and especially by yourself.

Overevaluation of your importance and competence can put you in a precarious position. The conceited person is generally disliked. Conceit with a haughty, arrogant, assertive manner implies an overevaluation of one's importance. The conceited person assumes a better-than-thou attitude.

Consider the case of a five-year-old girl, Mary. She came from a well-to-do family in a small town. She attended a school in which there were many foreign pupils. The foreign children could not speak or read or write or count very well; they were bashful, timid, backward, and lacking in self-confidence.

Years later, as a college student, Mary recalled her experience in that school:

> When a boy about ten years old would try to read he would stumble because he couldn't pronounce a word. I would raise my hand and fairly jump out of my seat to show the teacher that I knew how. I would laugh and feel superior to those big boys who were much older than me and still didn't know how to read.
>
> I thought that my father was superior to theirs because he didn't have to work in the lime quarry. After school I would take five or six children into the store with me and line them up in a row, and give each a piece of candy. I still can feel the delight and condescending manner I had when I did this. My father would tell my mother how unselfish I had been, which made me feel very proud of myself. But I think I liked the superior feeling it gave me.
>
> I imagined that all the children must be jealous of me and that they wanted to be like me. When my mother came to visit the school I felt so proud, because not many mothers came, as the foreign women couldn't speak English. When my teacher praised me I thought all the children looked at me enviously.

Comment on this case is hardly necessary. The social situation in that schoolroom was obviously unfair to all the children, including Mary.

Humility is the absence of a pride and overevaluation of oneself. The humble person evaluates his accomplishments realistically and if he errs, it is on the side of underevaluation. Humility does not imply submissiveness. Many of the greatest leaders have been described as humble. There is a danger in overhumility. Realistic self-evaluation means giving oneself credit appropriately.

Feelings of Embarrassment, Shame, Guilt, Remorse

Feelings of embarrassment occur in social situations. If you have made a fool of yourself in public or committed a *faux pas* or if you are caught in some questionable act, you are embarrassed because of the way you think you then appear to others.

If it is customary for the women of a tribe to conceal the face with a veil, a woman feels embarrassment or shame when caught with the face uncovered. Not too long ago it was considered indecent if a woman revealed her ankle! In some tribes the people wear no clothing and experience no shame over exposure of the genital organs. Yet Adam and Eve, it is said, acquired the dubious gift of shame or modesty, and made aprons of fig leaves! Among civilized peoples the exposure of the genitals is felt to be indecent and a source of embarrassment or of shame.

Children, as all mothers know, are born without a sense of shame, just as animals are. Before they can experience feelings of shame, they must learn what is considered proper and what improper within their social world. The conditions that induce shame—whether in the child, the primitive person, or the adult—vary with the mores of the group. At one time or another, all children have said something like, "Mom! I'd rather *die* than wear that!"

The evolution of the bathing suit, through the past two generations, illustrates well the changing mores in dress and exposure of the body, and changes in the conditions that produce feelings of embarrassment and shame.

Embarrassment arises when some social rule of conduct has been violated. Malinowski (1927), in his study of sex and repression among savage people, reports that among the Trobriand Islanders it is commonly believed that parents do not resemble their offspring and that children of the same parents do not resemble each other. It is taboo even to hint that a child resembles its mother or any of its maternal kinsfolk. When Malinowski commented upon the striking likeness between two brothers, there was a hush over the assembly; the brother withdrew abruptly and the company was half-embarrassed, half-offended at the breach of etiquette. In this instance a taboo influenced the perception of similarity and difference. And feelings of embarrassment arose from violation of the taboo.

Illustrations of situations that elicit shame could be multiplied indefinitely, from our own and primitive cultures. Inasmuch as sexual behavior is usually regulated by the mores of various cultures, sometimes frustrating a powerful instinct, it is not surprising that feelings of guilt and remorse should frequently arise in the area of sexual conduct.

Pullias (1937) studied the beliefs and feelings of boys and young men over the practice of masturbation. He describes a young man who had been taught that autoerotic practices are morally wrong:

> John is a boy eighteen years of age. During his fourteenth, fifteenth, and sixteenth years he masturbated habitually. Since then he has indulged in this activity only occasionally. He believes that one who has done "this deed" has degraded himself morally, and that such a person cannot succeed or prosper. All of his failures he explains in terms of this belief. He does not make a fraternity; it is because of his habit. He is not liked by young women. The explanation is simple: he has degraded himself. Thus the young man has lived for years in a state of resigned self-condemnation.

Pullias questioned seventy-five young men regarding their beliefs about masturbation. He found a rather widespread belief that it is physically, mentally, or morally damaging. Psychiatrists and psychologists today, however, believe that this is not true. But guilt feelings and anxiety may result from an inner conflict between a normal sexual urge and self-imposed (or socially imposed) standards of conduct. The mental conflict may be suppressed or repressed.

Feelings of guilt arise in various nonsexual situations. For example, if a man is caught cheating in an examination or at a game of cards, he feels ashamed of himself or guilty. If a child is accused of being cruel to an animal or mean to a younger child, he may feel guilty. And thieves, murderers, and other criminals, if caught in the act, may suffer from a sense of guilt; although some, sorry to be caught, appear to lack a "guilty conscience." There are many gradations and forms of these self-regarding feelings of embarrassment, shame, guilt, and remorse.

Remorse refers to a previous and persisting sense of guilt arising from past wrongs or misdeeds. It may be a lasting form of self-reproach. Remorse may lead to penitence—to sorrow for past faults and misdeeds—and to acts intended to relieve the remorse.

Abnormal Feelings of Guilt

There are persons who feel guilty when no one would condemn them. Consider the teenager who commits suicide because of his acute acne; the woman who cannot conceive because of guilt over one instance of premarital sex. Such individuals are in a mental state of conflict with standards of conduct and evaluation that are self-imposed and that may become largely unconscious. The true nature of a conflict may be unknown to the subject.

One patient in a psychopathic hospital was convinced that he had committed the "unpardonable sin." The exact nature of this sin was quite vague to him. Nevertheless, he appeared to be experiencing a profound sense of guilt and self-reproach. With head bowed and a despondent countenance he rocked back and forth in his chair, repeating over and over: "All the evil in the world I have done. I am responsible for all the sin and trouble in the world. I am to blame for it all. . . ." This patient was in an abnormal state of conflict and suffered a profound sense of guilt and remorse.

In contrast to this consider the person with a *character neurosis* who for some reason or other has failed to develop a normal sense of guilt. He is a psychopathic amoral person—perhaps a "heartless cad who loves 'em and leaves 'em," or a killer who tortures and kills with no apparent emotion. Long ago this would have been called *moral insanity*.

It is important that a child learn at an early age to know the difference between right and wrong. Parents have an obligation to train their children so that they will know the difference between good and bad actions. The church, too, helps in the development of conscience by teaching the child what he *ought* and *ought not* to do. During adolescence and maturity the law of the land specifies the difference between correct amd incorrect conduct and lays down the penalty for wrongdoing. Laws and customs differ from country to country, but the standards related to guilt and wrongdoing can be found everywhere.

Freud distinguished among psychological entities called the *id, ego,* and *superego.* For him the *id* consisted of blind, primitive instincts, especially those of sex and hostility that are largely unconscious. The *ego* is an agency that reconciles the claims of the *id* with reality, with environmental forces and with the *superego.* The *superego* is the ideal self with standards of correct conduct. The *superego* acts as a conscience, indicating to the *ego* what is right and wrong.

These agencies, according to Freud, are factors in human conflicts. The superego forces the ego to act in opposition to the id. The ego is subjected to pressures from both sides. The ego must reconcile the conflicting claims of id and superego. Beyond serving as umpire among the forces of the id, superego, and the environment, the ego acts as an executive agent—making decisions, setting goals, keeping promises, discharging obligations, avoiding catastrophic situations.

Through the decisions and actions of the ego the individual becomes in some measure an effective, reliable, relatively autonomous human being.

In the eyes of a physiological psychologist, the Freudian entities appear to designate hypothetical (perhaps mythical) agents. Yet no one will question the existence of biological impulses such as sex, hostility, hunger and thirst (id). Nor can anyone doubt the existence of social norms and standards of moral conduct. Such standards are accepted by the individual, internalized; they serve as a basis for evaluating conduct as right or wrong (superego). Nor will anyone question the psychological reality of conflicts between biological impulses and social ideals. Finally, there can be little doubt that to most individuals the concept of self (ego) is about the most important thing in the world. The self-concept enters as a factor into feelings of inferiority and superiority, feelings of love and hate, of sex, fear, anxiety, anger, resentment, hostility, and other feelings and emotions. This is true regardless of how psychologists define the self-concept.

I am not sure that feelings of shame and guilt are unique to man. When a dog or cat has been scolded for some misdeed—for example, urinating on the parlor rug—it may show a slinking, avoiding behavior when the master scolds it. It is quite easy to interpret such behavior as shame or guilt, even though we cannot know what the animal really feels.

Ego-Involvement and Identification

During the second year of life, when words begin to be used, the baby talks about himself in the third person. He says: "Baby wants ball," or "John wants milk." Personal pronouns *I*, *me*, *mine* develop later; the use of *we* comes later than *I*. Verbal references to the self are learned along with other words and by the same process of acquisition.

When a child refers to something as *mine*—whether a toy, a pet, a shoe, a parent, a house—there is said to be ego-involvement. The personal pronoun implies that the child has some knowledge of himself as an individual distinct from other individuals and things. A baby of two years was taken to the beach, where she ran to the water, spread her arms, and said her favorite word—"Mine"! The whole Atlantic Ocean!

The child claims some territory as his own. It may be a play yard, a room in the house, a bed, a school, etc. We know also that animals claim a territory as their own and defend it against intruders. Adults recognize certain places as their own. This is necessary and important in growth.

Sherif and Cantril (1947) have described it this way:

> The space may be some corner of a room where we have a favorite chair, it may be some glade in the woods to which we make recurrent visits, it may be a barrel in the woodshed we like to sit on in the evening after dinner. Whatever it is, we come to feel that that space is not only ours but it is a part of us. If it is pre-empted by someone else, destroyed, or intruded upon, *we* are annoyed, we feel that *our* privacy, *our* selves have been violated, injured or insulted.

A person becomes ego-involved with his or her family, automobile, home town, profession, church, political party, goals, and values. People are loyal to their own things and will defend them. Ego-involvement gives an emotional tinge to certain courses of action. It gives interest and vitality to pieces of property, systems of belief, plans for action, or whatever the individual accepts as belonging to himself.

Ego-involvement is a form of identification. As a psychological concept, however, *identification* has at least three meanings. First, a child is said to identify himself with its parents or with an older child or with some hero who serves as a model. Hero worship implies identification in this sense. Second, we identify ourselves with the characters on the stage or in a novel or TV show. We put ourselves in their place and vicariously experience their feelings. This has been called empathy. Third, identification means ego-involvement in the sense we have described above. A person is identified with his clothing, his automobile, his home, his club, and so on. These are *his* things.

Changes in the Self-Concept

The self-regarding beliefs, attitudes, values, and motives that an individual holds are the products of experience. The self is a *cognitive* construct that changes with age, experience, state of health, and environmental circumstances. The self is not a constant, but a variable construct. Your beliefs regarding yourself change with the perception of your personal and social situation.

Great transformations in the concept of self occur at the time of adolescence. With sexual maturity the changes in personality are so radical that it is correct to say that a new *self* has emerged from the old. The metamorphosis is like that of the butterfly emerging from the cocoon.

In times of stress there are sometimes pronounced changes in the self-evaluating attitudes and in personality. We say that a person "does not act like himself" or that "a different self has emerged."

During the Vietnam war, Americans taken prisoner attempted to preserve their independence and self-respect, but this sometimes became impossible with the brutal treatment of the Viet Cong. Some of the prisoners were subjected to horrible experiences that completely altered their personalities and self-definitions. In time, some of these men lost their old allegiances and identifications. In order to survive, they gradually accepted new allegiances and identifications that were more in conformity with the standards and practices of their captors. Some regressed to a childlike relationship in which they cooperated with the Viet Cong, took on their ideology, and continued an unhappy existence. Self-respect was gone. A new ego system emerged. In this situation there was a radical change in the perception, belief, and evaluation of the self. "Brainwashing" is a deliberate attempt to change attitudes and alter the ego systems.

Further examples of transformation in the definition of self can be found in persons suffering from some physical change because of alcoholism, disease, or major surgery. Under the influence of alcohol a serious and controlled individual may become jovial, uninhibited, free and easy with his remarks; we say he is a "different person." Disease or a radical operation can so alter an individual's self-evaluation that he no longer acts like the same person. Consider the change a teenager may undergo after an operation to make his once "outstanding" ears fit closely to his head. (Parenthetically, we might add that not all such plastic surgery or dramatic physical change has positive benefits. It is said that a once-obese person always thinks of himself as a "fatty," even after a huge weight loss. And if a person who has had a beautiful "nose job" has a thoroughly ingrained habit of self-deprecation, he may never *act* like the now-beautiful person he *is*.)

From the above and similar illustrations it is obvious that the definition and characteristics of the self vary with physical, biological, psychological, and social conditions. The characteristics of the self change with circumstances.

The self is a *cognitive* concept. It is not an entity, but a complex of beliefs, ideas, attitudes, and values that develop with experience and that change with age, health, and environmental circumstances.

The "self system" is an example of the major role that cognitive processes play in the determination of feelings and emotions. What you *feel*, what you say and do, even your mental health, all depend to a high degree on your perception, memory, imagination, evaluation of the surrounding world, and your relation to that world. Especially important are your relationships to other persons and your self-regarding attitudes.

EMOTIONAL PROBLEMS INVOLVING LOVE, HATE, AND SEXUAL MOTIVATION

The word *love* is commonly used in a broad sense to designate almost any kind of *liking*. Thus a man is said to *love* his home, his work, his religion, his smoking jacket and slippers, as well as his wife and children. All of us have heard about the small child who when asked to distinguish between *liking* and *loving*, replied: "I *like* my mother but I *love* ice cream."

In the psychological literature the term *love* is used in several senses to designate a mood, an emotion, an attitude, a motive, or a state of conflict. Obviously the term needs to be clearly defined when used by the psychologist.

In Webster's Collegiate Dictionary there are several definitions of *love*. Two, in particular, are relevant to the present discussion: "An unselfish concern that freely accepts another in loyalty and seeks his good." And, "The attraction based on sexual desire: affection and tenderness felt by lovers." Thus there are nonsexual and sexual forms of love.

The nonsexual form is described by such terms as *benevolence, attachment, devotion, admiration*. The nonsexual forms of love include love of parents for children and children for parents, love of brothers and sisters for each other, love of friends, love of mankind, love of God. The attitude toward a long-cherished pet is sometimes a genuine love attitude, too. Nonsexual love is made manifest by giving and receiving acts of kindness, helpfulness, and generosity. This is illustrated in the care and feeding of an infant by its mother, with the intimate physical contacts involved in nursing, bathing, dressing, and other care. Caressing and fondling figure largely in establishing love attitudes. There is also a sharing of playful behavior by parent and child.

In the sexual form of love the affectionate behavior is usually directed toward a member of the opposite sex. Commonly the relationship is a reciprocal one, each of the pair revealing, in behavior, love for the other. The factors mentioned above as bases of nonsexual love may or may not be factors in sexual desire. Caressing, kissing, and similar affectionate demonstrations play an important role in sexual love. It is said that the basis of sexual love is physical attractiveness and contact. The sexual appetite is aroused through the senses and is normally consummated in the complete sexual act.

An attitude that is opposed to love is that of hate. The term *hate* is commonly used in as broad a sense as *love*. The term is roughly equivalent to *dislike*. Thus a child will say, "I *hate* homework."

An attitude of hate may be based upon frustrations. If a dictator rules the country cruelly and in an overbearing manner, frustrating desires of the citizens for independence, security, freedom, and dignity, the citizens will come to hate him—i.e., they will develop attitudes of intense dislike and antagonism. In the sexual relation, the failure of a partner to give satisfaction to the mate, combined with other frustrations, may develop an attitude of indifference or hatred of the sexual partner. Hate is a *negative* attitude and feeling. Love is *positive*.

Attitudes of Liking and Disliking

What makes us like certain persons and dislike others? What traits of personality, what actions, remarks, physical appearance, and the like induce *positive* attitudes and what induce *negative*? Are there sex differences in the factors that determine liking and disliking persons? These questions were studied with college students by Thomas and Young (1938).

The subjects were 676 students in an elementary psychology course at the University of Illinois. Each student was given a printed form which instructed him to list in one column the initials of a few persons who were the *most liked*, and in another column the initials of a few who were the *most disliked*. The sex of each person listed was also indicated on the blank. The rank order of persons *liked* and persons *disliked*, from most to least, was indicated on the blank. There was provision that two or more persons could be given the same rank.

Analysis of results showed that, on the average, 2.7 more persons were listed in the column headed *like* than in the column headed *dislike*. This was true for both sexes. Also, the persons whose initials were listed tended to be of the same sex as the person who did the listing—a fact that indicates that your friends and acquaintances tend to be of the same sex as yourself. The person ranked as *most highly* liked, however, was usually a person of the opposite sex. This fact is not surprising for college students in the mating years.

But times have changed since this study was made. Young people are much more "non-sexist" (to use a term that is common today) in their choice of companions than they used to be. This is having an effect on such things as college dorms, marriage relationships, and strict sex roles. Women are entering the business world and professions demanding the same privileges and pay as men. A "best friend" no longer necessarily implies a romantic relationship.

TABLE 2
Alleged Reasons for Liking Persons

| Why women *like:* | | | | Why men *like:* | | | |
| WOMEN | | MEN | | MEN | | WOMEN | |
Trait	N	Trait	N	Trait	N	Trait	N
intelligent	134	intelligent	154	intelligent	130	beautiful	129
cheerful	123	considerate	102	cheerful	101	intelligent	90
helpful	103	kind	79	friendly	91	cheerful	56
loyal	101	cheerful	70	common interests	90	congenial	55
generous	94	mannerly	70	congenial	87	sex-appeal	53
sweet	84	conversational	62	helpful	83	friendly	46
entertaining	84	handsome	61	loyal	78	kind	46
kind	82	sense of humor	61	sense of humor	70	good sport	41
good sport	79	congenial	55	generous	64	helpful	31
common interests	77	interesting	54	good sport	50	considerate	29

| Why women *dislike:* | | | | Why men *dislike:* | | | |
| WOMEN | | MEN | | MEN | | WOMEN | |
Trait	N	Trait	N	Trait	N	Trait	N
conceited	111	conceited	122	conceited	170	conceited	48
deceitful	73	selfish	33	self-centered	48	gossips	31
selfish	70	unmannerly	30	unintelligent	46	snobbish	25
loud	43	overbearing	27	deceitful	42	deceitful	21
self-centered	40	deceitful	24	overbearing	37	unintelligent	20
snobbish	40	uninteresting	22	dishonest	37	loud	16
affected	32	unintelligent	21	selfish	35	selfish	16
unmannerly	32	self-centered	19	loud	33	affected	14
overbearing	31	untruthful	19	snobbish	32	silly	14
inconsiderate	28	boastful	16	unmannerly	32	talkative	14

On the second page of the printed form the students were instructed to give the reasons for liking and disliking the persons they had listed. In Table 2 are listed the ten most frequently mentioned traits that lead to liking and disliking persons and the frequency with which each trait was mentioned. Inspection of these lists shows that both sexes agree well on the alleged reasons for liking and disliking persons. The tabulation speaks for itself and needs no special comment.

Jealousy

Jealousy is a state of conflict that arises from situations that threaten the love, care, or attention received from a parent or lover.

Such frustration by a rival lover normally leads to attack upon the intruder. The attack may be physical, as when one attempts to injure or kill the rival; or the attack may take a more subtle substitute form, as when sarcastic words are used.

In modern polite society we no longer have duels and bouts with swords. An overt attack upon a rival is taboo. Consequently, a jealous person may substitute slanderous or deprecating remarks. He may maneuver the rival into appearing disadvantageously before the object of his love; or in more subtle ways he may reveal an attitude of hostility toward the rival lover.

Sexual jealousy has its biological counterpart among various animal species. During the mating season, males commonly fight for possession of a female. For example, during the mating season the female elephant seals climb out of the sea onto the rocky beach and await the arrival of the males. When two or more dominant males arrive, there is often a life-and-death struggle for possession of the harem. The strongest and fittest males leave offspring; the weakest are eliminated in the struggle. Darwin pointed out that the antlers of the deer, the spurs of the cock, the superior size and strength of most male animals, have developed in the vital struggle for mates as well as defense of self, mate, offspring, and territory.

There is also a gentler side to sexual selection. The beautiful plumage of the male peacock, pheasant, and other birds have evolved to charm or entice the female. According to Darwin, the female selects the most attractive and charming male, who in turn becomes the father of an oncoming generation. Through sexual selection in mating, a type of male is developed which is increasingly attractive to the female of the species, and increasingly equipped for survival in life's struggle.

Jealous behavior commonly appears in the human family when another baby is born. The attention, care, and affection of the mother are now diverted from the older child to the newcomer. The jealous child may respond by making an attack upon the baby. For example, consider the case of Joseph, a six-year-old boy, described by Foster (1927):

> He was born while his father was overseas during the first World War. At that time the mother made her home with relatives. She frankly admits that she showered affection and caresses on the baby, filling her life with the baby's needs in order not to think about the possible fate of his father. When the baby was a year old the father returned. Upon entering the home he greeted the mother demonstratively, paying no attention at the

moment to Joseph. The baby showed a temper which could not at once be quieted. For a long time after this he resented the affectionate attention which was shown to his mother by the father. Noting this, both parents adopted the practice of including him in their demonstrations of affection. When another son was born, Joseph again showed marked jealousy and on several occasions tried to injure him, once throwing a steel tool from the automobile kit at him. To overcome this the parents tried to see that both shared alike in everything. But at the present time, if Richard is ill and receives special attention, Joseph produces a cough or some other symptom that brings him attention also.

If the object of desire is property or position or honor belonging to someone else, rather than love and affection, the terms *envy* and *covetousness* are appropriate. For example, a man would like to own the beautiful new automobile in which Mr. Neighbor rides. His wife desires a fur coat as elegant as the one Mrs. Neighbor wears. Their son wants a bicycle like that of Jimmy Neighbor. These persons are covetous and envious but not jealous (in the above sense).

Romantic Love

The state of "being in love" is an emotionally disturbed state which may last for an indefinite period. The lovers are more or less activated sexually but also to some extent they are inhibited.

Mutual caressing arouses the lovers. Physical contacts—holding hands, dancing, kissing, embracing, petting—are sexually arousing. The normal biological completion of love-making is sexual union. But in our culture, sexual union outside of wedlock has traditionally been taboo. The taboo is based on the likelihood of pregnancy and the birth of a child without a legal father and suitable home conditions for its rearing. Most young people in the past have been deterred from sexual promiscuity by knowledge of this danger and fear of social ostracism if an unwanted and illegitimate baby is born. Lovers may have a fear of pregnancy, of venereal diseases, of social ostracism. There are also moral and religious teachings about good and bad conduct and the sanctity of the home. All of these sex-inhibitory (negative) influences tend to heighten the state of conflict for premarital or extramarital lovers.

It is true that sexual morality has changed a great deal with the advent of the pill, with modern medicine, and a new sense of freedom in personal relations. Views concerning love, marriage, and the home are changing. But problems regarding the care of children and mental health and happiness remain despite current changes in the mores.

In romantic love the lovers are typically both sexually aroused and sexually inhibited. The more strongly they are aroused by sexual stimulation and the more completely the biological urge is frustrated, the greater will be the emotional disturbance.

Of course, there are varying degrees of "being in love." A girl may tell a friend that she is "in love" with her history teacher, even though he scarcely knows who she is. Or a couple may be "in love" and lucky enough to possess an emotional maturity and stability that allows this state to continue for years of a happy union. A couple that has been married for twenty years may claim to love one another but say that they were "in love" only during their courtship and early marriage years. Love means many things to many people, and there is no one all-encompassing definition, but the state of being "in love" usually assumes a disturbed emotional state, a "romantic" condition in which conflict exists.

Various circumstances can complicate the conflict state of romantic love. One of the lovers may become suspicious or have knowledge that there is a rival; this introduces an element of jealousy. Again, signs of disinterest on the part of a lover may make the outcome of the romantic relation uncertain and produce anxiety. Usually the self-evaluation of both lovers is strongly involved. There may or may not be feelings of guilt. Each lover identifies himself with the other and becomes proverbially blind to the other's defects.

The conflict of "being in love" is resolved in various ways. In marriage there are attitudes of trust, loyalty, and confidence in the fidelity of the partner. Attitudes of love remain but with little or no conflict. Of course, infidelity in marriage can produce an intense conflict state which is not very romantic. This kind of conflict may lead to separation, divorce, and sometimes to violence. Motivations in this kind of conflict may be, in part, subconscious or unconscious.

Romantic love, as everyone knows, may end unhappily. The conflict state of "being in love" may turn into indifference or hatred with separation and desertion by one of the partners. Loss of love may bring persistent unhappiness, loneliness, and a lowering of self-esteem. Poets and novelists, however, have filled literature with stories of true and lasting love. Romantic love can be happy while it lasts. And for some lucky few it lasts a long time.

The Loss of Love

The loss of love can bring negative emotions. The specific form of conscious feeling that is aroused depends upon the cognition, the beliefs and attitudes, of the losing person and his perception of the external situation.

Loss of love can occur in various ways. A lover may desert his mate for another. In this case the consciousness may be tinged with jealousy or with resentment or hatred. The feeling depends upon the way the subject perceives and understands the situation, the way he looks at things. Again, the loved one may become ill and die. In this situation there is normally a feeling of sorrow and grief at the loss.

The death of a mate eliminates habitual forms of sexual satisfaction. But bereavement involves much more than sorrow for this loss. There is a loss of someone to talk to, loss of companionship, loss of someone to share work with, to help in various ways, etc. If the death of a loved one or friend is sudden and unexpected, there is an emotional shock. In rare cases a neurosis develops. For example, there was a widow whose only son died. For years she kept his room intact and preserved everything that reminded her of him. Her actions preserved the sense of loss. She tried not to forget.

The affective reaction depends upon the way the person perceives and understands his situation. Adjustment requires a re-evaluation of the situation.

With animals, the separation of an infant from its mother produces a profound reaction in the young one. The infant monkey, for example, cries and makes searching, agitated reactions. Substitute mothering may relieve the distress, the extent of relief depending upon the kind of substitute mothering and on the nature of the tie to the original mother. If there is no substitute, the infant becomes quiet and depressed. The reaction is somewhat similar to that observed with unfortunately bereft children.

In general, perception and cognitive awareness of the inducing situation determine the pattern of feelings and emotions when there is loss of love. And perception is relative to the dispositions (beliefs, attitudes, values, motives) already established by experience. Everything depends upon the way you look at things.

Sexual Motivation and Emotion

The sexual appetite (desire, lust) is a potent form of human motivation, similar in many ways to the sexual motivation observed in nonhuman animals. Animals show patterns of courtship, mating, gestation, birth, nursing, and care of the young.

The sexual appetite of both sexes, when uninhibited, normally leads to sexual union. During preliminary stages of sexual play the level of excitement rises until ejaculation occurs in the male and a physiological equivalent occurs in the female. The orgasm marks the climax of the sexual appetite, for the time being, through appetitive satisfaction. Appetites are cyclic and tend to recur.

From the subjective point of view, the sexual act is normally pleasurable. This basic fact insures the carrying on of the species. Normal intercourse leaves a relaxed, contented mood. But sometimes the orgasm is not attained and a state of nervous tension and excitement remain. Failure to achieve a complete orgasm may lead to such things as the growth of indifference about sex, or attitudes of resentment and hatred of the partner, or feelings of inadequacy.

Today a great deal of research and therapy is concerned with achievement of satisfying sexual relations. Frigidity in women and impotence in men are often based upon ignorance and attitudes toward sex that were developed during premarital years. A woman's sexual responses may be inhibited because of an early sex experience. A man may have anxiety concerning his masculinity. With help and guidance, such conditions can often be corrected and sexual relations achieved. Counseling and therapy are available.

Elsewhere I referred to the views of Hardy (1964) on the role of hedonic processes in the organization and development of the sexual appetite. (See page 81.) There can be no doubt that positive and negative affective processes play a dominant role in human sexual development and behavior.

What is a sexual emotion? The answer obviously depends on how you choose to define emotion.

If you take the broad definition and equate emotion with all affective processes, then sexual excitement and relief are clearly emotional events. However, the appetites for air, water, food, elimination, sleep, rest, activity, and others, are rarely regarded as *emotional,* although affective tones are definitely involved. Appetitive behavior and emotive behavior can be, and usually are, distinguished. What is the difference?

Ordinarily we speak of *feelings* of hunger, thirst, and other appetitive states. These states originate in internal bodily conditions of disturbed homeostasis. Emotions, contrastingly, originate in situations that involve the relationship between organism and environment. Emotions have a broader cognitive basis.

If you follow the view that emotion is a disturbed affective state of psychological origin, then sexual activity is emotional to the extent that disturbance of experience and behavior is involved. From this point of view, there can be no doubt that such states as jealousy, romantic love, loss of love, lust, and the like are emotional disturbances. They are *sexual* emotions insofar as sexual motivations are aroused and frustrated, in conflict, or satisfied.

In any event, the problem of defining emotion is less important than gaining a true understanding of the nature of psychological reality.

FEAR AND ANXIETY

The concept of fear covers a variety of specific forms of emotion which have one feature in common: the presence of a danger or threat. The nature of the danger may be obscure at the time fear arises, or it may even be imaginary. The threat may come from the environment in the form of an unexpected event or from a perception which conflicts with expectation or with something valued. The reaction to the threatening situation is one of defense and preparation for action.

It will be helpful to consider different forms of fear and anxiety.

Startle and Fright

Startle is an innate reaction induced by loud sounds (such as the BANG of a gun), a sudden shock or jar to the body, loss of support, an unexpected fall, sudden movement in the visual field, a flash of light, and other unexpected stimulations.

We are all familiar with the quick muscular jerk or contraction of the body which occurs as a reaction to a sudden loud noise. The startle pattern is a general skeletal reflex which is over in one- to two-tenths of a second. As described by Landis and Hunt (1939), the startle pattern begins with blinking of the eyes and spreads quickly throughout the body to the extremities. There is forward movement of the head, a characteristic facial expression with opening of the mouth and closing of the eyes. The shoulders are raised and drawn forward. High-speed motion photography shows that the startle reaction spreads from head to extremities.

Landis and Hunt regard the startle pattern as a general skeletal reflex. Startle is not an emotion, they say, because the visceral processes controlled by the autonomic nervous system do not get underway until the startle reflex is over. Startle, however, commonly leads to observant behavior and often to a true emotional (visceral) response.

Startle occurs so quickly that the individual does not have time to identify the source of danger. With fright, however, there is a disturbance which is elicited by perception or cognizance of some sign of danger. Startle is a reaction to sensory stimulation. Fright involves *cognition* even though the nature of the threat is not clearly understood. We are frightened by situations that are unusual and potentially dangerous.

Young children are usually frightened by such things as thunder and lightning, barking dogs, reptiles, ghosts, death, and strange persons. When a stranger enters the house a small child may timidly hide behind his mother's skirts.

The objects and situations that elicit fright clearly change with age and with the development of understanding and control of the environment. (See Figure 11, page 79.)

Ability to control the situation diminishes or eliminates the fear. For example, a person who is afraid of the water may be carefully taught how to handle himself in the water. Gradually he will lose his fear as he learns to swim.

With adults there are rational grounds for fear. Earthquakes, floods, fires, volcanic eruptions, collisions, cyclones, and tornados present real dangers. Most adults have well-grounded *attitudes* of fear of these threatening conditions.

There are degrees or intensities of fright. Terror is an extreme reaction of fear that occurs when one is confronted with a real danger and does not know how to escape. A man trapped in a burning building may try to act wisely and calmly but he may "lose his head" and become terrified. A person confronted by a bandit with a gun, or in a house that is collapsing in an earthquake, may become terrified. There is little he can do. Frustration of the ability to escape heightens the emotional disturbance.

If a man faces danger without manifest fear, we say he is courageous. Courage is the anti-fear (fear-inhibitory) attitude.

Anxiety and Conflict

A highly important member of the family of fear emotions is anxiety. Anxiety is an enduring fear based on the anticipation or expectancy of harm. Anxiety is a conflict state. It is often complex.

There are mild degrees of anxiety and persisting intense forms. For example, a person visits the dentist. He hears the grinding of a tooth and anticipates a wicked pain. He is apprehensive and mildly anxious. But in the more serious affairs of life he may be threatened by disaster. He may anticipate financial failure. He is threatened by an impending divorce that he does not want. There is illness in the family that may prove to be fatal. In these and other serious situations a person's basic values are threatened. He is in a state of conflict and may develop an anxiety neurosis.

Anxiety is an inner threat rather than an immediate threat from the environment. The inner conflict may be suppressed or repressed, unconscious. In certain phobias, for example, the individual is not aware of why he or she is afraid. A person may suffer a great anxiety about flying, and not be aware of the reasons for this persistent fear.

In other cases, the cause of the anxiety may be remembered. One particular woman is frightened when enclosed in an elevator or in a train that enters a tunnel or another enclosed space. This claustrophobia originated in a well-remembered traumatic experience in China. When seriously ill, she was carried by coolies over a mountainous path in a palanquin (a coffin-like box) to a riverboat. The experience, especially because it concerned illness, was frightening and the anxiety conflict remained.

Severe emotional problems, as we said, can be damaging to health and possibly bring on a nervous breakdown. Crile (1915) described the case of a broker who was in sound health until, during a financial panic, his fortune and those of others were in jeopardy for almost a year. His business finally failed. During the long strain, with constant anxiety, he became increasingly nervous. Gradually he developed a pulsating enlargement of the thyroid gland, an increased prominence of the eyes, marked increase in perspiration, palpitation of the heart, more rapid respiration with frequent sighing, and an increased blood pressure. There were tremors in fingers and other groups of muscles, a loss of weight and strength, frequent gastrointestinal disturbances, and a loss of normal control of impulses to act. He was broken in health as truly as in fortune. His symptoms followed in the wake of intense anxiety. Such symptoms, in good part, are psychogenic. They can sometimes be removed by psychotherapy. (See page 113.)

The striking benefits of good luck, success, or happiness; of change of scene; of relaxing pursuits; of optimistic and helpful friends are explained by the psychogenic hypothesis—the hypothesis that feelings and emotions have somatic (bodily) effects.

One often hears the advice "don't worry," but this is easier said than done. The submariner during a war who, with the crew, is awaiting a depth bomb that could bring disaster, can do nothing about the situation. He does worry. But in many other situations an understanding and re-evaluation of the cause of anxiety can help. Control of the situation can remove or mitigate anxiety but this is not always possible.

Consider, however, the plight of the anxious person whose anxiety rests not upon external dangers but on the tug of war between inner motivations. A woman may be both a talented singer and a devoted mother. While she is on a concert tour she feels anxious about the welfare of her children, guilty about being absent. While she is at home busy in domestic and maternal chores, her desire to sing nags at her. She is in a state of severe mental conflict. Let us hope that, with or without help, such a person will be able to solve the emotional problem, relieve the anxiety, and work out a way of living that is happy and productive.

ANGER, AGGRESSION, AND VIOLENCE

Fear and anger are perhaps the two most commonly mentioned emotions, although weeping in grief, laughing in joy, and lust are close competitors. Fear and anger are widespread throughout the animal kingdom. Both reactions are related to defense and attack in the strenuous struggle for survival and in maintaining a place in the pecking order. Nature has provided animals with means of defense and offense. Consider the lion's teeth and claws, the snake's fangs, the deer's antlers, the bird's spurs, the kangaroo's powerful muscles, all of which aid in a flight or a fight.

The flight from danger and threatening conditions is dynamically opposed to facing the situation with an attitude of attack and fight. Both reactions are clearly essential for survival in the vast realm of nature. The lion and other carnivorous animals depend upon capture and killing of their prey for food. The antelope and other ruminants of the plains depend upon speed in running to escape from predators.

In man, anger is associated with aggression, violence, destruction. A quarrel among children (or adults) may end in a fight. There may be a vocal exchange of deprecating words which becomes louder and louder. Tempers rise and the quarrelers come to blows. An angry person can become destructive, breaking furniture and other objects. He can attack, injure, or even kill his antagonist.

On the social level, the result of a quarrel can be a strained or broken interpersonal relation. Persons who have had an altercation may stop communicating in any way if a hostile, antagonistic frame of mind persists.

It took millions of years of organic evolution to develop man's present body-form including neural structures for defense and offense. It is not likely that recent refinements of civilization can greatly change man's biological constitution. Thus we can expect a certain amount of strife even among the most civilized people.

Anger and Frustration

An early study by Gates (1926) considered the many annoyances, irritations, aversions, and frustrations with which life is filled.

Gates instructed a group of fifty-one college women to keep records for a period of one week of their experiences of irritation and anger. Among the specific causes of anger were unjust accusations, insulting remarks, criticisms, contradictions, scoldings, unwelcome advice, work left undone, not being invited to a party, disobedience of children, being locked out, money lost, sleep interrupted, hunger, physical pain, etc.

This sample of common annoyances, irritations, and minor frustrations could be extended indefinitely. Gates reported that *persons* rather than *things* were the cause of anger in 115 out of 145 instances. The thwarting of an impulse to self-expression was frequently mentioned as a cause of anger. Insulting remarks lower the level of self-esteem and arouse anger and feelings of resentment. This factor of self-regard was clearly implicated in many feelings of anger.

Anger was sometimes felt with no impulse toward overt aggression. However, Gates reported the following impulses during anger: to make a verbal retort, pinch, shake, strike, choke, push, step on, scratch, shoot, beat, kill, tear to pieces, spank, break inanimate objects, etc. This list of reactions to frustration agrees with our previous statement that frustration and interruption of planned behavior normally lead to feelings of anger and aggressive behavior. (See page 99.)

The list also is compatible with the finding that as an infant develops into early childhood he becomes increasingly retaliative when painfully stimulated or frustrated. Anger, in fact, is first recognized and distinguished from general excitement by retaliative behavior. (See page 76.)

The situations that produce frustration change with age and experience. Symonds (1946) has described the sources of frustration at different stages of the life cycle:

Restricting of exploratory behavior. The normal infant brings things to his mouth; he grasps, touches, pulls, manipulates them. Parents find it necessary to restrict these activities to prevent injury, disease, fire. Inhibitions are imposed; these are frustrating to the normal exploratory activity of the infant.

Restriction of early sex experiences. The infant explores his world, including different parts of his body; he finds that manipulation of the genital organs yields pleasant feelings. Parents, in our culture, are usually alert and vigorous in thwarting expressions of autoerotism. The frustrations centering around masturbation are reacted to with strong emotion, fantasy, and repression.

Rivalries within the family. When another baby is born, the interest of the mother is diverted to the newcomer. The loss of attention and care is definitely frustrating to older children. Again, if two children want to play with the same toy, one child (perhaps the younger and weaker) must give it up, and this is frustrating.

Early feeding frustrations. Children brought into guidance clinics are frequently found to have had unsatisfactory nursing experiences. Perhaps they were weaned too soon or had unsatisfactory bottle feeding. Weaning is a prototype of later forms of frustration.

Loss of love and support. If both parents are absent often or if the home is broken, there may be a widespread frustration bound up with loss of love, security, and support. The frustrations from loss of love have a profound effect upon personality development of the child.

Cleanliness training. Toilet training is a frustration of early childhood. It is also frustrating to most children to have to wash the hands, brush teeth, and generally to keep clean.

Lessening dependence on the parents. As a child grows up he is expected to do more and more things for himself, to require less attention and care. The child is definitely frustrated by being forced to depend upon his own resources rather than upon the care of parents.

Frustrations from the school. In the schoolroom the child is required to sit still, to restrain from speaking and even whispering, to restrain from temper displays, to take care of materials in an orderly and clean manner. He is regimented to fit into the school situation. In addition to these thwartings, he is frustrated by failure in his work, through competition with superior pupils, and in other ways.

Adolescent frustrations. The adolescent must abandon childhood dependence for adulthood. He must acquire skills and attitudes for work. He must adjust himself to members of the opposite sex and to companions of his own sex. These adjustments involve repeated frustrations.

Adult frustrations. Economic necessity requires that the male adult earn a living and support a family. In times of high taxes or economic depression this involves marked frustrations. The professional man or woman maintains a status within his or her profession, club, and community, but not without repeated frustrations. Again, there are deprivations from death, financial failure, and other losses, that are severely frustrating.

In other words, from the cradle to the grave, people experience repeated frustrations, but their form and nature vary from one period of life to another. We do not escape frustrations by growing up. We just grow into new and different kinds of frustration. It is how we *handle* frustration that largely determines both our happiness and our success within our world.

Individual and Group Aggression

In an early study of motivation, Maller (1929) compared the effectiveness of working for personal gain versus working for social gain. Using school children as subjects, he found that working for personal, individual gain was decidedly more effective than working for a group score as a member of a group. He found that competing for oneself against a fellow worker yielded results far better in quantity and quality than working for a group as a member of that group. Self-interest dominated altruism, at least in this experiment.

In some cases, however, people may be strongly identified with their group. In football, for example, each individual player "fights" for the victory of his team. The crowd of onlookers is divided in loyalty. Each team has supporting spectators who cheer when a touchdown has been made by *their* team and are sober when *their* team is defeated.

Individuals belong to various groups. A person may be a member of a family, a community, a nation, a church, a club, etc., all at the same time. A person is identified with the groups to which he belongs. He will defend *his* groups and "fight" aggressively for them. Sometimes the interests of different groups conflict, and this must be resolved. A person may be a member of a church that forbids birth control for instance, and yet share with his or her marriage partner a strong desire to limit the size of the family. In this case, the loyalty to the family entity may win out over that to the church codes.

On the international scene, loyalties based on nationality, language, race, and religion are opposed to a rather weak and diffuse loyalty to world government and to mankind—to *homo sapiens*. In this basic fact lies a danger for all human beings. Loyalty to your labor union, nation, race, or religion commonly may dominate loyalty to mankind. You will act against opposing groups. Frustration and conflict of interests between groups can lead to aggression and violence—to strikes, or to war. It appears that, human nature being what it is, this is not likely to change much. However, as through communication, and improved transportation, the world becomes smaller, human beings are obviously going to have to consider the fate of civilization and include a concern for mankind as a whole in their loyalties.

War dances, pep meetings, political rallies, religious revivals, and the like are not rational proceedings. Such gatherings are aimed at arousing enthusiasm and strengthening group morale for a specific purpose. The level of arousal is heightened. Members of a group are prepared for action which can result in group aggression.

Although violence is *not* a necessary and inevitable outcome of individual and group aggression, behavior can become violent in mob action, riots, strikes and warfare. Police action may be needed to "keep the peace." In daily life we have become accustomed to reading about murder, arson, rape, kidnapping, hijacking, fighting, and wars. Violent behavior is indeed part of the contemporary human scene.

Ideological Frustrations

A system of ideology becomes tinged with feeling and urgency whenever an individual is strongly identified with it. Denial or contradiction of the ideology can produce acute frustration and conflict with resulting hostility. Consider a few examples: Parents in West Virginia have trained their children to believe that the biblical story of creation is literally true. Now textbooks are placed in the public schools that stress the scientific view of evolution as opposed to the doctrine of special creation. The parents vigorously protest the use of these books in the schools because they are inconsistent with religious beliefs.

A group of Indians living in the tropical forests of Brazil have a stone-age culture even today and are hostile toward the *civilizados* who are constructing a highway through *their* territory. Their way of living is so incompatible with twentieth-century civilization that frustration is inevitable.

American Indians have been driven off *their* land and placed on reservations. Their customs and ideology are threatened. They have become strangers in the midst of a foreign culture. They are hostile toward their non-Indian masters.

In these and many other examples that might be mentioned, infringement and contradiction of *my* beliefs, *my* rights, *my* property, *my* people—i.e., *my* ideology and way of life—are the source of frustration, anger, and persisting hostility.

Social Changes and Problems

My life began in the horse-and-buggy days of Los Angeles. I can recall the first electric light, the first telephone, the first automobile, the first airplane, the first electric streetcar, the first radio, the first TV, not to mention the jet airplane, the computer, space travel, and much more. During my lifetime there have been marvelous advances in science, engineering technology, and the medical arts. All of this has been called progress. What is progress? There have been revolutionary social and cultural changes but man's biological nature remains much the same as it has been through countless centuries.

There are urgent problems. There are exploding human populations in different parts of the world. The world's food supply has not kept up with population growth so that there is famine and starvation in many areas. There is also an energy crisis. The supply of oil on this globe is limited, while the growth of population and industrialization create an exponential increase in the demand for petroleum. At the same time there is pollution of air, water, ground, as mankind copes with the problem of survival in an increasingly complex world.

I have lived through two World Wars. Now there is talk about World War III with nuclear destruction of civilization, city by city. Wars are based on frustrations and conflicts of political, moral, and religious interests. Conflicts build up emotional tensions.

How can we deal with these pressing social problems? There is no pat answer. Understanding a situation from all possible points of view helps, but even with understanding, the situation may resemble that of two dogs and one bone. Usually the stronger dog gets the bone. With human problems, however, negotiation and compromise are often possible. Man has the advantage of being able to utilize cooperation, which is a superior method to competition and a struggle to the death. Cooperation as well as competition exists in the natural world. But law and order, justice and tranquility have to be achieved. They are not instinctive. All of man's abilities are called upon to bring about even a small amount of harmony and peace.

Human Nature and Emotion

According to the rationalist philosophy, man was regarded as a reasoning, thinking animal with freedom of choice. To achieve complete rationality, it was necessary to minimize and control the "baser" emotional elements of human nature so reason could dominate action. The rationalist regarded emotions as built-in reactions to natural surroundings. Reason was regarded as a superior, God-given faculty characterized by reflection and responsible choice.

The rationalist philosophy persists in the psychology of common sense and daily life, but a sharp dichotomy between reason and emotion is no longer tenable. Cognitive and affective processes cannot be sharply separated. Both are interrelated and together determine the pattern of action.

On the conscious level, feelings and emotions fuse with beliefs and ideas thus presenting a unity of experience. At times, of course, there are emotional frustrations, conflicts, interruptions, states of confusion and distraction from the smooth flow of thought and action. Emotional diffusiveness—crying, screaming, swearing, laughing—is a common occurrence. These disturbances are marked by the awareness of widespread bodily changes in smooth muscles and glands and by felt impulses to action.

On the cerebral level, there is commonly an integration of neural activity expressed in smooth, ongoing behavior. When frustration, conflict, and intense stimulation are present there is a temporary "excortication." Signs of disturbance are acutely felt as viscereal processes that are controlled by the autonomic nervous system, as we saw in an earlier chapter.

Any view of human nature that ignores the basic biological and social nature of man, that fails to accept man's sometimes irrational, emotional behavior, is nearsighted and potentially disastrous. We might wish that human nature were different; but a wish does not change biological and psychological reality.

MOTIVATION, EMOTION, AND ADJUSTMENT

The words *motivation* and *emotion* are derived from the same Latin root, *movere*, which means *to move*. In the literal sense of the word, whatever moves the organism is motivating, whether it be a physical stimulus or a conscious intention. Painful environmental stimulations and internal feelings of discomfort such as hunger are, broadly considered, motivating. Emotion, when regarded as a pattern of bodily movement, is motivated.

There are psychologists who insist that the process of motivation is always goal-oriented, purposive, and directive, *as well as* activating. Motivated behavior, they argue, is directed toward the fulfillment of some plan, purpose, or motive. Desires, such as the seeking of food, and all specific intentions to act, *are* motives.

Positive and negative affective arousals are motivating in that they are both activating and directive. A positive affective process leads the organism to perpetuate and later to reproduce the conditions that elicit it. A negative affective arousal leads the organism to terminate and later to avoid the conditions that produce it. Affective processes, therefore, are both activating and directive. They are motivating and regulatory.

When choice is possible between two responses to sensory stimulations, the stimulation producing the more intense positive affective arousal (or the less intense negative arousal) dominates and determines the choice. A test of preference shows the relative potency of two motivations.

Since emotions are observed as movements of the organism, a question can be raised as to whether we need two terms, *emotion* and *motivation*, to describe and analyze behavior. Emotions, of course, are more complex than simple reflexes. Emotions are elicited by cognitive processes. They are based on perception and understanding of the situation in which a person finds himself. But from an objective point of view, emotions are observed as complex bodily movements.

I have assumed that *all behavior is motivated* in the sense of being causally determined. The determinants can be viewed from different standpoints: physically, biologically, psychologically, socially. All behavior is activated, motivated. Some behavior is purposive, goal-oriented, directed, organized. By definition, some behavior (emotional) lacks an apparent goal. But the development of purposive behavior out of aimless activity can be readily observed.

Mental Conflicts

When a psychologist speaks of *mental* states—perceptual dispositions, personality traits, social attitudes, intentions, habit structures, abilities, skills, emotional dispositions, and the like—he is interpreting facts of human experience and behavior. *Mental* states and processes are not logically opposed to physical. Mental determinants, like physical, are inferred.

Although dualists talk as if mind and body were distinct entities, the view of biological monism does not warrant a real dichotomy. Mind and body are one. There is a single individual underlying conscious experience and behavior. When this individual is examined from the point of view of conscious experience the term *mental* is used. The term just indicates one line of approach to the study of determinants that exist within individuals.

Affective arousals leave mental traces. Threats of impending danger leave a mental state of anxiety. Outbursts of anger are well remembered; they leave an impression on the mind which underlies feelings of resentment and hostility. Experiences of love and hate leave persisting dispositions within the mind. There are hopes and fears, likes and dislikes, and specific expectancies that originated in conscious experience and persist for an indefinite time.

Unresolved conflicts influence feelings and emotions. Freud demonstrated that childhood hostilities can be repressed into an unconscious complex. A child, for example, can be angered and hostile toward a punitive parent but the child is small and helpless; he has learned that overt aggression against the parent brings punishment. To avoid punishment he suppresses hostile aggression. The mental conflict is repressed and becomes an unconscious state. Not only hostility but threats to one's self-esteem, frustrated motives of love and sex, fears, and other experiences are commonly forced into the realm of the unconscious mind. Under some conditions there is loss of sleep, irritable behavior, neurosis which may produce physical symptoms.

There is a "hidden self" that underlies a person's feelings and emotions. A man may cover up his sorrow with a grin and not be aware of the psychological nature of the sorrow. He may have anxiety resting on a conflict of which he is only partly conscious. He may suppress loves and hates, resentments, hostilities, hopes, fears, and expectations which rarely surface into clear consciousness.

Mental conflicts can indeed lead to unhappiness. They may lead to failure in interpersonal relations. There is often a need for help in re-evaluating a situation, for solving an emotional problem, and for reorienting one's outlook on life.

Adjustment

Adjustments to disorganized mental states can be made through trial-and-error learning, by direct attack upon the frustrating object, by avoidance and escape, by substituting one goal for another, by changing an attitude, or by re-evaluating the situation and acting accordingly. Some forms of adjustment are called *defense reactions* because they protect your self-esteem. Rationalization, projection of blame, belittling others, all are techniques for saving face. Sometimes they solve no problem and should be called pseudo-adjustments. Displaced aggression does not really solve any problem. It may make you *feel* better, but it does not change the objective situation.

Clinical psychologists, psychiatrists, counselors, and others commonly describe adjustment in evaluative terms. According to one definition, adjustment is a *satisfactory relation of an organism to its environment.* The meaning of this definition hinges upon the evaluative word *satisfactory.* Again, adjustment has been defined as *adaptation to the demands of reality. Adaptation,* implying an element of fitness or suitability, is an evaluative term. A good adaptation favors survival; a poor adaptation interferes with survival of individual or species. According to another definition, adjustment is an individual's *relationship to his environment which is necessary for him in order to live comfortably and without strain and conflict.* This definition, like the others, is evaluative. Further, it implies that feelings of comfort and discomfort play a part in making adjustments. When you speak of a maladjustment you imply a standard of evaluation: health, happiness, biological survival, physiological and/or emotional homeostasis or something else.

Adjustment has been described as a process of problem solving, of restoring equilibrium, returning from disturbance to complacency, reducing drive, reducing emotional tension, removing persisting negative stimulations, minimizing distress and maximizing happiness. These phrases imply that motivation is an underlying factor in adjustment. They also imply that there is a *direction* in the process of making an adjustment.

It is possible to describe adjustment objectively in nonevaluative terms as a change in the relation between an organism and its environment. The change may be in the organism or in the environment or in both. In an emotional situation you can change your attitude or change your environment in some way.

Facts and Values

Philosophers have argued that science deals with facts and not with values. Despite this distinction, men of science have been much concerned with problems that involve values. Values, in some sense or other, are determinants of human activity. Values are closely related to attitudes, interests, specific intentions. These and closely related psychological processes are based upon feelings and emotions in their origin and development.

I have argued that evaluative behavior can be observed with animals as truly as with human beings. Accepting a food is a positive evaluation; rejecting it, a negative evaluation. Preference is relative evaluation implying that one reaction is better in some way than another. (See page 40.)

If we regard behavior as evaluative, we can observe evaluative reactions in animals and human beings. Evaluative behavior then becomes a matter of observed fact and a scientific axiology, to some extent, becomes possible.

If we are strictly mechanistic, we can avoid the postulate of evaluative and estimative behavior in nonhuman animals. Even Darwin's view that some emotional expressions have biological utility, however, implies that there is a prime value of life—simply to survive. Similarly, the view that emotion is a disturbed process or state—a disorganization or perturbation of intentional behavior—is evaluative. This view carries the implication that emotion is harmful, undesirable, or useless. From a philosophical point of view we can say that one reaction dominates another or that the "preferred" reaction is superior to the "nonpreferred."

In the practical affairs of living, however, evaluations are inevitable. Parents, teachers, ministers, propagandists, men of science, and others instill in children and youths ideas of good and bad, right and wrong, good taste and bad taste, truth and error, beauty and ugliness, etc. We evaluate many things: musical performance, paintings, political ideas, traits of character, the quality of foods, services, and so on. We cannot escape evaluative reactions.

The man of science may claim that his research is matter-of-fact and value-free. But despite this claim he values truth, logical consistency, integrity, and clarity of statement. These are intellectual values which are distinct from economic, political, aesthetic, moral, and religious values. There are different standards of evaluation.

In daily life, decisions are necessary when different courses of action and different policies appear to be possible. Choice is influenced by existing attitudes, interests, sentiments, and related dispositions. Self-interest may dominate altruism.

The story is told of Abraham Lincoln who, as a youth, saw slaves being sold on the New Orleans market. He was emotionally disturbed by what he saw and said, "If ever I have the chance, I will hit that thing hard." At the time the emotional disturbance was useless, but the negative reaction changed Lincoln's attitude toward slavery and formed his character and life purposes. A later decision to free the slaves may have been partly determined by this evaluative attitude. The attitude influenced human history.

As we can see, then, our emotions and feelings are in effect the ways by which we respond to, see, evaluate life situations. They are part of our lives. How we have learned to react determines our adjustment, or lack of it, to the world around us. What we do—the way we love, hate, accept, reject, prefer—depends on our feelings and emotions. A great deal depends upon the way we look at things.

Appendix I. Animal Studies of Food Preference, Appetite, and Habit

Preference for Foods as Relative Evaluation

An example of preferential hierarchies is presented in Figure A-1. In this illustration letters symbolize the following foods:

M = fresh milk standardized at 4% butterfat

S = granulated cane sugar, extra fine

W = whole wheat powder, freshly ground

D = dehydrated milk—a commercial product known as KLIM (which is milk spelled backwards)

F = commercial white flour made from wheat

B = pure butterfat prepared for the experiment

Preferential Hierarchies of Ten Rats Tested with Six Foods

Rat	Preferential Hierachy									
40	S	>	M	>	W	>	D	>	B	>	F
41	M	>	S	>	W	>	D	>	B	>	F
42	M	>	S	>	D	>	W	>	F	>	B
43	M	>	S	>	D	>	W	>	F	>	B
44	M	>	S	>	W	>	D	>	B	>	F
45	M	>	S	>	W	>	D	>	F	>	-*
46	M	>	S	>	W	>	D	>	B	>	F
47	M	>	S	>	W	>	D	>	B	>	F
48	M	>	S	>	W	>	D	>	F	>	B
49	M	>	S	>	W	>	D	>	F	>	B
Group	M	>	S	>	W	>	D	>	F	>	B

*Died before B vs F test.

Figure A-1. Preferential hierarchies of ten rats tested with six foods. From Young (1933).

The implication in this experiment (see Chapter 3) is that the foods arrange themselves naturally into a transitive series from low to high levels of acceptability or hedonic value. The hierarchies of acceptability are relatively stable when dietary and testing conditions are constant. There are individual differences in preference, for example, between M and S, W and D, F and B, shown in Figure A-1. But these differences are between test foods that are close together on the group preferential hierarchy.

The Hedonic Equivalence of Different Stimuli

Studies by Young and Madsen (1963) demonstrated the hedonic equivalence of solutions of sodium-saccharin and sucrose. For a sodium-saccharin solution of constant concentration it is possible to determine the concentration of an hedonically equivalent sucrose solution. The method, known as the up-and-down psychophysical method, requires that the concentration of sucrose in a series of solutions be varied up and down during repeated trials in a test of preference. From the accumulated data it is possible to compute the sucrose concentration that is isohedonic to that of the constant saccharin solution.*

The hedonic equivalence function is shown in Figure A-2. Vertical lines crossing the curve indicate the range of individual measures of hedonic equality for a group of eight rats tested individually. The solid curve is the mean hedonic-equivalence function for the group as a whole. On the basis of this curve I estimated that the optimal concentration for solutions of sodium-saccharin is located at about 0.5 grams per 100 ml (milliliters) of solution. This optimal value is hedonically equivalent to a sucrose solution with concentration of about 3.5 grams per 100 ml of solution. Incidentally, human observers report that sodium-saccharin solutions are sweet and pleasant up to a concentration of about 0.5%; higher concentrations become sharp (bitter?) and unpleasant.

---

* For statistical details of the up-and-down method see: W. J. Dixon and F. J. Massey, Jr. (1957). In preference tests with this method, the subject is offered a choice between a standard and a comparison solution. The sucrose concentration of the comparison solution is varied up and down in a series of trials. From the data, an average sucrose concentration is computed which is isohedonic to the standard concentration.

The up-and-down method has one limitation when used in studies of hedonic processes. The method implies a normal distribution of hedonic values above and below a standard level. Actually, because hedonic effects are reinforcing, every choice may influence following choices. Under these conditions we may not assume a normal distribution of hedonic values. Nevertheless, the method has been useful in psychophysical studies of affective processes.

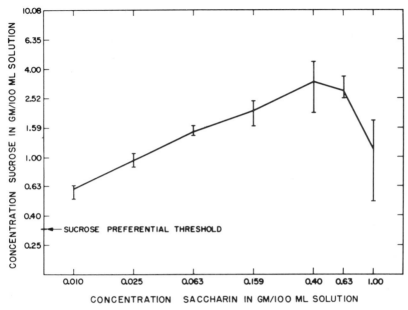

Figure A-2. The hedonic equivalence function for solutions of sodium-saccharin and sucrose. From Young and Madsen (1963). The curve is based on preference tests with a group of eight rats.

The curve shows, as a reference point, the sucrose preferential threshold (0.32) as determined by Burright and Kappauf (1963), who used a method based on choice. This is the concentration at which rats begin to discriminate preferentially between sucrose solutions and distilled water.

Sensory and Hedonic Integration

Hedonic integration follows an algebraic principle of summation which is different from the integrating of sensory properties. For example, solutions containing sucrose are hedonically positive to rats, and solutions containing quinine are hedonically negative. If compound solutions are prepared that contain both sucrose and quinine, the positive and negative hedonic values summate algebraically. A bitter-sweet compound, therefore, has an hedonic value that varies with the concentrations of the two solutes.

Figure A-3 shows a stimulus area which represents an infinite

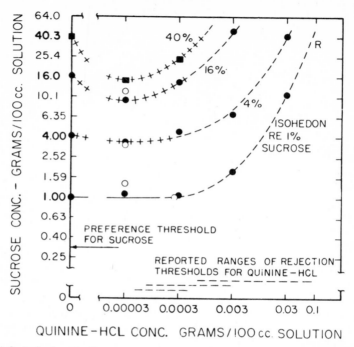

Figure A-3. Isohedons in the sucrose-quinine stimulus-area. From Kappauf, Burright and DeMarco (1963).

number of compound solutions containing two solutes: sucrose and quinine hydrochloride. Each point in the area represents a bitter-sweet compound.

In an experiment by Kappauf, Burright and DeMarco (1963), four standard sucrose solutions were used for hedonic comparisons with bitter-sweet compounds. By varying the sucrose concentration (sweetness) of the compound up and down on successive trials it is possible to compute from the data the sucrose concentration in the compound that makes it isohedonic with the standard.

An isohedon is a curve plotted in a stimulus area. All points on a curve are hedonically equal to a standard sucrose solution. In Figure A-3 four isohedons are plotted with four sucrose standards.

Kappauf et al. found that extremely low concentrations of quinine in the compound enhance palatability. This fact is represented by a series of + signs. Higher concentrations of quinine in the compound impair palatability. This is represented by a series of − signs. In the experimental literature the rodent's response to quinine hydrochloride is reported as uniformly negative, aversive. It is an interesting fact that these extremely low quinine concentrations enhance palatability. They are below the recognition threshold for quinine.

Similar isohedons have been plotted in the following stimulus areas: sucrose-sodium chloride, sucrose-saccharin, sucrose-quinine hydrochloride, sucrose-tartaric acid. In all these stimulus areas, low concentrations of the nonsucrose component enhance palatability and higher concentrations impair palatability. Hence there is algebraic summation of hedonic intensities.

Food Preferences in Relation to Habit and Nutritional Need

With nonhuman animals, palatability, the pleasantness or unpleasantness of contact with foods, determines choice. Palatability can be demonstrated within a strictly objective frame of reference. See Young (1967b). With nonhuman animals there are also deferred beneficial or detrimental effects that, through memory, can become associated with the ingestion of particular foods. If an animal associates the ingestion of a particular food with a positive beneficial effect or with relief from a negative detrimental effect, a dietary habit becomes established. If the deferred hedonic effect is negative, as with the ingestion of toxic substances, aversive behavior develops. The hedonic effects regulate the selection of foods at the intraorganic level as well as at the oropharyngeal level. As an example of simultaneous dual preferences consider the following experiment:

J. P. Chaplin and I (1945) maintained groups of rats in large cafeteria cages upon an eleven-component self-selected Richter diet. Every animal in the group had unlimited access to the eleven dietary components which were presented in separate containers. Two of these components, selected for experimental study, were sucrose (cane sugar, a carbohydrate and source of energy) and granular casein (a protein which is necessary for normal metabolism and growth).

At the start of the experiment all rats were given a brief-exposure preference test with the test foods side by side and positions alternated from trial to trial. Rats were offered a choice between sucrose and casein. Preference tests were repeated at different stages of the experiment. The tests showed conclusively that the sweet-tasting sucrose was preferred to casein. For some reason or other casein is low in palatability.

A metabolic and nutritional need for protein was then created by removing casein from the cafeteria maintenance cages. Protein starvation steadily increased day by day. Despite a growing need for protein, the animals developed and maintained a preference for sucrose when tested with the brief-exposure technique. After twenty-nine days of protein starvation, the need for protein was severe and obvious, but the rats increasingly developed and maintained a preference for the sweet-tasting sugar.

At this stage of the experiment another method of testing preference was employed. The test foods were widely separated as in a T- or Y-maze. At the choice point the foods were out of range of the head receptors; foods could not be seen or touched or smelled or tasted. Each rat made a series of runs, being forced to choose between a run-to-sucrose or a run-to-casein.

Under these conditions all animals promptly and consistently developed a running-to-casein preference. The reward for a choice was a brief nibble of the incentive food on every round trip.

For a while we could demonstrate two simultaneous and incompatible preferences! When tested with the brief-exposure foods-together apparatus the rats preferred sucrose. A few minutes later, when tested on the apparatus with foods in fixed, widely separated positions, they consistently chose the casein—a choice in agreement with their obvious metabolic and nutritional need.

The existence of simultaneous incompatible choices requires an explanation. After a tedious series of control experiments we conclude that the preference for sucrose was a *habit of choice* that had developed on the basis of relative palatability. The opposed preference for casein was based upon an intraorganic effect: relief from the distress produced by protein starvation. Relief from distress is an hedonic change away from the negative pole of the hedonic continuum and toward the positive pole.

The general principle revealed by the experiment is this: *Habits of choice tend to form in agreement with metabolic and nutritional needs, but an established habit may persist even though opposed to bodily needs.*

The Stabilizing Role of Food Habits

During the early years of vitamin research, L. J. Harris and his co-workers (1933), in England, performed some interesting experiments upon the self-selection of diets by laboratory rats. These workers maintained rats on a basal diet which could be made inadequate by withdrawal of the vitamin-B complex. The rats developed avitaminosis when the vitamin-B complex was withdrawn. They were then offered a choice among six or more foods, differently flavored, only one of which contained the needed vitamin in a small but sufficient amount.

Records of intake showed that the rats were unable to select the vitamin-containing food on the basis of flavor. Avitaminosis developed.

At this stage of the experiment the rats were "educated." Their "education" consisted of being offered the vitamin-containing food for two or three days, without choice, until they could experience the curative and beneficial effect of the diet and associate this effect with the characteristic flavor of the food.

When the "educated" rats were again offered the original choice, they continued to select the food containing the needed vitamin. Then the vitamin was transferred to a food with a different flavor. The rats, however, continued to select the food that previously had contained the vitamin. Avitaminosis again developed. But Harris and his associates found that it was possible to "re-educate" the rats. The animals would then continue to select a different vitamin-containing food.

These early experiments are important for two reasons. First, they imply that relief from the distressing condition of avitaminosis favors development of a dietary habit. This is an hedonic change. Second, they demonstrate the stabilizing influence of habits on the selection of foods.

The Roles of Hedonic Processes and Exercise in Behavioral Development

In an early study with the brief-exposure preference technique, I observed preferential trends and shifts in preference (Young, 1933). In every test sugar (sucrose) was a constant standard. The comparison foods (in order of testing) were flour, wheat, butterfat, and milk. See the preferential hierarchies in Figure A-1 (page 149).

Figure A-4 shows the percent of choices made for each pair of test foods by a group of three male rats. Percentages greater than 50 percent indicate the preferred food.

Inspection of this figure reveals several outstanding principles:

1. In every sequence of tests there is a consistent preference. Sugar is preferred to flour, to wheat, to butterfat. Milk is preferred to sugar.

2. In every sequence of tests there is a preferential trend—i.e., a more or less steady increase in the percent of choices of the preferred food. The trend shows the gradual development of a preferential habit with repeated exercise in discrimination. The slope and shape of the

trend depend upon the *difference* in palatability between the test foods and possibly also upon dietary conditions.

3. When one test food is substituted for another there is an abrupt shift in the percent of choices. These abrupt shifts are motivational. They indicate a dynamic difference in affective arousal by the two incentives.

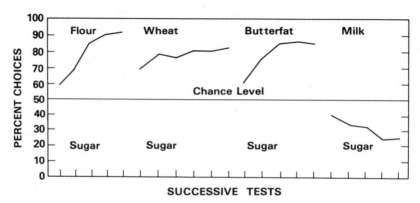

Figure A-4. Percent choices of sugar (sucrose) tested for preference against flour, wheat, butterfat, and milk during successive blocks of tests. From Young (1933).

4. The more gradual trends indicate learning. They show the cumulative influence of practice, or repetition, of a choice with incentives that have different hedonic values.

Affective Arousal and Development of Cognitive Expectations

Preference tests with sugar solutions have shown that rats prefer the higher concentration (the sweeter) to the lower (less sweet). For example, with sucrose solutions the preferential hierarchy is: $32\% > 8\% > 4\% > 1\%$.

In an experiment by C. L. Trafton, four groups, each of eight naive rats, were given opportunity to ingest sugar solutions presented singly without the possibility of choice and preference. The experiment is reported by Young (1966, p. 79).

The rats were tested individually. Those in one group were offered a sugar solution of 1 percent; those in other groups were offered solutions of 4, 8, 32 percent, respectively. The solutions were licked at the tip of a nozzle projecting into the testing cage. Separate licks (contacts with a solution) were counted electrically during a daily exposure period of 60 seconds. This procedure was followed for eleven days. Then all rats were offered an incentive of distilled water for five additional days.

The results of this experiment are shown in Figure A-5. The results indicate that during the first presentations the mean rate of licking was directly proportional to the sucrose concentration. During the first five days (apart from two minor inversions on day 3) the mean numbers of licks per minute were proportional to the sucrose concentrations. This fact is important because it shows that the preferred solution is more highly activating, motivating, in terms of tongue responses, than the nonpreferred.

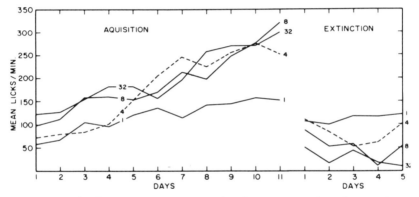

Figure A-5. Levels of tongue activation as related to concentration of sugar (sucrose) solutions during successive stages of habituation. Plotted from data of Dr. C. L. Trafton, reported by Young (1966). The curves show mean licks per minute during acquisition and extinction.

Throughout the first eleven days the rate of licking steadily increased for all solutions as the rats became increasingly habituated to the experimental situation. There was less and less exploratory activity and more and more time given to licking the solutions.

It will be noted, however, that the curve for the 1 percent group remains relatively low, while the curves for the other groups after day 5 cross and recross in a random manner and do not differ significantly from each other. This is due to the fact that the rats, with practice, approached a physiological limit to the rate of licking. They tended to lick all sweet solutions at a maximal rate.

After eleven days of acquisition, all animals were offered, in the same nozzle, an incentive of distilled water. The result is shown by the curves during five days of extinction. For all rats the substitution of distilled water for a sucrose solution brought an immediate decrease in the rate of licking. The 1 percent rats showed the *least* change in level of tongue activation and the 32 percent rats showed the *greatest* change. After five days of extinction, the mean rates of licking were inversely proportional to the initial sucrose concentrations and to the initial levels of tongue activation. The performance during extinction is clearly a function of the *difference* (discrepancy) between the concentrations and distilled water (o percent).

Two conclusions can be drawn from this instructive experiment. First, it is *sucrose* in solution (pleasantness) that motivates the licking. When the sucrose is withdrawn and distilled water substituted, there is a marked decline in tongue activation. Second, during repeated exposures to a sucrose solution the animals developed an *expectation*. The 32 percent animals learned to expect a very sweet solution. The 8 percent and 4 percent animals learned to expect a less sweet solution; and the 1 percent rats learned to expect a solution that is just a little sweet.

These expectations were acquired through experience and are cognitive in nature. The results during extinction cannot be explained in terms of stimulation alone, since all animals received the same stimulation (distilled water). Only an *acquired expectation* (habit) can explain the result. The inversion of licking rates during extinction can be explained only in terms of previous experience. But a detailed explanation of this phenomenon is lacking.

Appendix II. The Bodily Basis
of Feelings and Emotions

You cannot fully understand feelings and emotions without an elementary knowledge of the human nervous system. Consequently, a brief review of the principal structures and functions of the nervous system will be helpful at this point.

The main divisions are: (1) The *central nervous system,* located within the vertebral column and skull (cranium). This system includes the spinal cord and the brain. (2) The *peripheral nervous system* is composed of nerves that go to various organs and structures throughout the body. Some fibers in the peripheral system are *afferent,* carrying impulses from sense organs into the central system. Other fibers are *efferent,* carrying impulses away from the central system to muscles and glands. (3) The *autonomic system* regulates the muscles and glands that control homeostasis and function during feelings and emotions. The two main divisions—the *sympathetic* and *parasympathetic*—will be considered in detail below.

The unit of all nervous structures is the *neuron,* or nerve cell. There are millions of neurons in the human body. Neurons are in contact at the *synapse,* a place where excitations are transmitted from cell to cell by electrical and chemical changes.

THE AUTONOMIC NERVOUS SYSTEM

The autonomic nervous system regulates the bodily changes that outwardly express feelings and emotions. Figure A-6 is a diagram of the autonomic system and the bodily structures that it serves.

From the point of view of structure there are three main divisions: (1) The *cranial* division is made up of fibers emerging from the central nervous system at the base of the brain in several cranial nerves. These nerves (represented by broken lines) carry impulses outward to ganglia where synapses are formed with other neurons (represented by solid lines) that excite the smooth muscles and glands shown at the right of the figure. (2) The *thoracicolumbar* division is a network of fibers

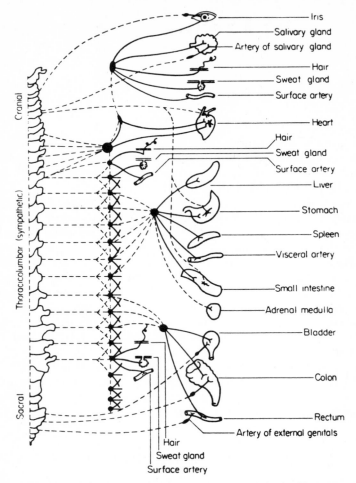

Iris
Salivary gland
Artery of salivary gland
Hair
Sweat gland
Surface artery
Heart
Hair
Sweat gland
Surface artery
Liver
Stomach
Spleen
Visceral artery
Small intestine
Adrenal medulla
Bladder
Colon
Rectum
Artery of external genitals
Hair
Sweat gland
Surface artery

Cranial

Thoracicolumbar (sympathetic)

Sacral

Figure A-6. Diagram of the autonomic nervous system and the bodily structures that it serves.

with nerves emerging from the spinal cord at the thoracic and lumbar levels. The nerves of this division form a network that responds as a unit producing widespread bodily changes. (3) The *sacral* division is composed of fibers emerging from the central nervous system at the sacrum, or pelvic region.

From the point of view of function there are two (not three) main divisions of the autonomic nervous system. The thoracicolumbar division, when considered from the physiological point of view, is commonly designated as the *sympathetic nervous system*. This system is a vast network of fibers producing widespread bodily changes in smooth muscles and glands as shown in Table 1-A. The upper (cranial) and

TABLE 1-A
Autonomic Functions

Sympathetic Nerves	Bodily Structures	Parasympathetic Nerves
		Cranial
Dilates the pupil	Iris	Constricts the pupil
Inhibits secretion	Salivary glands	Facilitates secretion
Erects (pilomotor reflex)	Hair	
Augments secretion	Sweat glands	
Constricts	Surface arteries	
Accelerates	Heart	Inhibits
Dilates bronchioles	Lung	Contracts bronchioles
Secretes glucose	Liver	
Inhibits gastric secretion and peristalsis	Stomach	Facilitates gastric secretion and peristalsis
Constricts, giving off erythrocytes	Spleen	
Secretes adrenin	Adrenal medulla	
Inhibits smooth muscle activity	Small intestine	Facilitates smooth muscle activity
Constricts	Visceral arteries	
		Sacral
Relaxes smooth muscle	Bladder	Contracts smooth muscle (empties)
Relaxes smooth muscle	Colon and rectum	Contracts smooth muscle (empties)
Constricts, counteracting erection	Arteries of external genitals	Dilates, causing erection
Contracts at orgasm	*Vasa deferentia*	
Contracts at orgasm	Seminal vesicles	
Contracts at orgasm	Uterus	

lower (sacral) divisions together constitute the *parasympathetic nervous system*. *Para* means "along the side of" or "beside." This designation is appropriate because the parasympathetic nerves are anatomically beside the sympathetic and, to a considerable extent, innervate (positively or negatively) the same structures.

The sympathetic and parasympathetic nerves are functionally

antagonistic and reciprocally related. This means that when the sympathetic nerves excite, the parasympathetic nerves inhibit, and vice versa. This reciprocal relation can be seen in Table 1 by comparing sympathetic and parasympathetic effects on the bodily structures.

The sympathetic network responds as a unit to produce various bodily changes. The parasympathetic nerves, in contrast, produce particular effects upon specific organs. Thus the third cranial nerve constricts the pupil, cutting down the amount of light that enters the eye. The seventh and ninth cranial nerves reach out to the salivary glands, to the mucous membranes and, through ganglia, to the tear (lacrimal) glands. The tenth cranial nerve (vagus) has a widespread distribution to the heart, lungs, stomach, liver, pancreas, and intestine. The pelvic nerves supply the colon, rectum, bladder, and external genitals. The particular effects of the parasympathetic nerves combined with the diffuse action of the sympathetic system produce a variety of visceral patterns of response during emotion.

THE LIMBIC SYSTEM

Deeply embedded at the very center of the brain is a system of neural structures of major importance in the regulation of feelings and emotions. This is known as the limbic system.

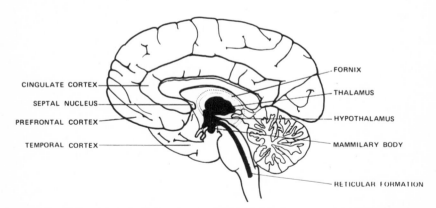

Figure A-7. The limbic system, a medial sagital view. From John L. Weil, *A Neurophysiological Model of Emotional and Intentional Behavior.* Courtesy of Charles C Thomas, Publisher, Springfield, Illinois (1974).

The main parts of the limbic system and their technical anatomical names are shown in Figure A-7. Some of these structures will be referred to when we consider the physiological theories of emotion. Different parts of the limbic system are interconnected. The functional relations between parts of the limbic system and the relation of this system to the cerebral cortex are matters that are at the forefront of current investigation by scientists. (See Weil [1974].)

Chemical Regulation

Pribram (1967a, 1967b) pointed out that core structures at the intermediate neural level are sensitive to a variety of chemical agents. Receptor sites have been identified that are sensitive to estrogenic steroids, circulating glucose, some amino acids or derivatives, osmotic equilibrium of electrolytes, androgenic and adrenal steroids, acetylcholine, epinephrine, and the partial pressure of CO_2. There is probably also a center that is sensitive to sodium. These chemical agents play a major role in regulating homeostasis. The chemical agents, circulating in the blood stream, act upon specific targets and produce specific effects.

Bibliography

ANGIER, R. P., "The Conflict Theory of Emotion," *American Journal of Psychology*, 39 (1927), 390–401.

ARNOLD, M. B., *Emotion and Personality: Vol. I, Psychological Aspects, Vol. II, Neurological and Physiological Aspects.* New York: Columbia University Press, 1960.

AX, A. F., "The Physiological Differentiation between Fear and Anger in Humans," *Psychosomatic Medicine*, 15 (1953), 433–42.

BARD, P., "The Neurohumoral Basis of Emotional Reactions," in C. Murchison, ed., *A Handbook of General Experimental Psychology.* Worcester, Mass.: Clark University Press, 1934.

BEEBE-CENTER, J. G. *The Psychology of Pleasantness and Unpleasantness.* New York: D. Van Nostrand Co., 1932.

BRIDGES, K. M. B., "A Genetic Theory of the Emotions," *Journal of Genetic Psychology*, 37 (1930), 514–27.

———, *The Social and Emotional Development of the Pre-School Child.* London: Kegan, Paul, Trench, Trubner, & Co., 1931.

———, "Emotional Development in Early Infancy," *Child Development*, 3 (1932), 324–41.

BURRIGHT, R. G., and W. E. KAPPAUF, "Preference Threshold of the White Rat for Sucrose," *Journal of Comparative and Physiological Psychology*, 56 (1963), 171–73.

CABANAC, M., "Physiological Role of Pleasure," *Science*, 173 (17 September, 1971), 1103–1107.

CAMERON, N., and A. MAGARET, *Behavior Pathology.* Boston: Houghton Mifflin, 1951.

CANNON, W. B., "The James-Lange Theory of Emotions: A Critical Examination and An Alternative Theory," *American Journal of Psychology*, 39 (1927), 106–24.

———, *Bodily Changes in Pain, Hunger, Fear and Rage: An Account of Recent Researches into the Function of Emotional Excitement*, 2nd ed. New York: Appleton-Century, 1929.

————, "Again the James-Lange and the Thalamic Theories of Emotion," *Psychological Review*, 38 (1931), 281–95.

————, *The Wisdom of the Body*. New York: Norton & Co., 1932.

CARR, H. A., *Psychology: A Study of Mental Activity*. New York: Longmans, Green & Co., 1925, pp. 287–308.

CRILE, G. W., *The Origin and Nature of the Emotions*. Philadelphia: Saunders, 1915.

CULLEN, J. W., *Legacies in the Study of Behavior: The Wisdom and Experience of Many*. Springfield, Illinois: C. C. Thomas, 1974.

CULLER,. E. A. K., *Motor Conditioning in Dogs*, film from the animal hearing laboratory at the University of Illinois. Distributed by C. H. Stoelting Co., 1350 S. Kostner Ave., Chicago, Ill., 60623.

DARROW, C. W., "Emotion as Relative Functional Decortication: The Role of Conflict," *Psychological Review*, 42 (1935), 566–78.

DARWIN, C., *The Expression of the Emotions in Man and Animal*. London: John Murray, 1872.

DELGADO, J. M. R., W. W. ROBERTS, and N. E. MILLER, "Learning Motivated by Electrical Stimulation of the Brain," *American Journal of Physiology*, 179 (1954), 587–93.

DIXON, W. J., and F. J. MASSEY, JR., *Introduction to Statistical Analysis*. New York: McGraw-Hill, 1957.

DOLLARD, J., L. W. DOOB, N. E. MILLER, and R. R. SEARS, *Frustration and Aggression*. New Haven: Yale University Press, 1939.

FOSTER, S., "A Study of the Personality Make-Up and Social Setting of Fifty Jealous Children," *Mental Hygiene*, 11 (1927), 53–77.

GARDINER, H. M., R. C. METCALF, and J. G. BEEBE-CENTER, *Feeling and Emotion: A History of Theories*. New York: American Book Co., 1937.

GATES, G. S., "An Observational Study of Anger," *Journal of Experimental Psychology*, 9 (1926), 325–36.

GLASS, D. C., ed., *Neurophysiology and Emotion: Proceedings of a Conference under the Auspices of Russell Sage Foundation and the Rockefeller University*. New York: The Rockefeller University Press, 1967.

GOODENOUGH, F. L., *Anger in Young Children*, University of Minnesota, Institute of Child Welfare Monograph Series, No. 9. Minneapolis: University of Minnesota Press, 1931.

GRINKER, R. R., and J. P. SPIEGEL, *Men Under Stress*. Philadelphia: Blakiston, 1945.

GROSSMAN, S. P., *A Textbook of Physiological Psychology*. New York: John Wiley & Sons, 1967.

GUTHRIE, E. R., *The Psychology of Human Conflict: The Clash of Motives Within the Individual.* New York: Harper & Brothers, 1938.

HARDY, K. R., "An Appetitional Theory of Sexual Motivation," *Psychological Review*, 71 (1964), 1–18.

————, "Sexual Appetite and Sexual Drive: A Reply," *Psychological Reports*, 17 (1965), 11–14.

HARRIS, L. J., J. CLAY, F. J. HARGREAVES, and A. WARD, Appetite and Choice of Diet. The Ability of the Vitamin B Deficient Rat to Discriminate between Diets Containing and Lacking the Vitamin, *Proceedings of the Royal Society of London, Series B (biological sciences)*, 113 (1933), 161–90.

HART, B., *The Psychology of Insanity*, 4th ed. New York: Macmillan Co., 1937.

HAYWORTH, D., "The Social Origin and Function of Laughter," *Psychological Review*, 35 (1928), 367–84.

HEATH, R. G., "Pleasure Response of Human Subjects to Direct Stimulation·of the Brain: Physiologic and Psychodynamic Considerations," in R. G. Heath, ed., *The Role of Pleasure in Behavior: A Symposium by 22 Authors.* New York: Harper & Row, Hoeber Medical Division, 1964, pp. 219–43.

HEBB, D. O., "Emotion in Man and Animal: An Analysis of the Intuitive Process of Recognition," *Psychological Review*, 53 (1946), 88–106.

————, "Drives and the C.N.S. (Conceptual Nervous System)," *Psychological Review*, 62 (1955), 243–54.

HENLE, M., "E. B. Titchener and the Case of the Missing Element," *Journal of the History of the Behavioral Sciences*, 10 (1974), 227–37.

HILLMAN, J., *Emotion: A Comprehensive Phenomenology of Theories and Their Meanings for Therapy.* Evanston, Illinois: Northwestern University Press, 1961.

HODGE, F. A., "The Emotions in a New Role," *Psychological Review*, 42 (1935), 555–65.

HOLLINGWORTH, L. S., *The Psychology of the Adolescent.* New York: Appleton-Century, 1928.

HUNT, J. McV., M. W. COLE, and E. S. REIS, "Situational Cues Distinguishing Anger, Fear, and Sorrow," *American Journal of Psychology*, 71 (1958), 136–51.

IZARD, C. E., *The Face of Emotion.* New York: Appleton-Century-Crofts, 1971.

JAMES, W., *The Principles of Psychology*, Vol. II. New York: Holt, 1913. (First edition 1890.)

JERSILD, A. T., and F. B. HOLMES, Children's Fears, *Child Development Monographs*, No. 20, 1935.

KANNER, L., "Judging Emotions from Facial Expression," *Psychological Monographs*, 41, No. 3 (1931).

KAPPAUF, W. E., R. G. BURRIGHT, and W. DeMARCO, "Sucrose-Quinine Mixtures which are Isohedonic for the Rat," *Journal of Comparative and Physiological Psychology*, 56 (1963), 138–43.

KENDERDINE, M., "Laughter in the Pre-School Child," *Child Development*, 2 (1931), 228–30.

KINSEY, A. C., W. B. POMEROY, and C. E. MARTIN, *Sexual Behavior in the Human Male*. Philadelphia: W. B. Saunders, 1948.

KNIEP, E. H., W. L. MORGAN, and P. T. YOUNG, "Studies in Affective Psychology: XI, Individual Differences in Affective Reaction to Odors, XII, The Relation Between Age and Affective Reaction to Odors," *American Journal of Psychology*, 43 (1931), 406–21.

KONORSKI, J., "Study of Behavior: Science or Pseudoscience," in J. W. Cullen, ed., *Legacies in the Study of Behavior*. Springfield, Illinois: C. C. Thomas, 1974.

LANDIS, C., "Studies of Emotional Reactions: II, General Behavior and Facial Expression," *Journal of Comparative Psychology*, 4 (1924), 447–501.

LANDIS, C., and W. A. HUNT, *The Startle Pattern*. New York: Farrar & Rinehart, 1939.

LEEPER, R. W., "A Motivational Theory of Emotion to Replace 'Emotion as Disorganized Response,'" *Psychological Review*, 55 (1948), 5–21.

LINDSLEY, D. B., "Emotion," in S. S. Stevens, ed., *Handbook of Experimental Psychology*. New York: John Wiley & Sons, 1951.

————, "Psychophysiology and Motivation," in M. R. Jones, ed., *Nebraska Symposium on Motivation*. Lincoln, Nebraska: University of Nebraska Press, 1957.

LUND, F. H., "Why Do We Weep?" *Journal of Social Psychology*, 1 (1930), 136–51.

LURIA, A. R., *The Nature of Human Conflicts, or Emotion, Conflict and Will*, trans. from Russian by W. H. Gantt. New York: Liveright, Inc., 1932.

MALINOWSKI, B., *Sex and Repression in Savage Society*. New York: Harcourt, Brace & Co., 1927.

MALLER, J. B., "Cooperation and Competition: An Experimental Study in Motivation," *Columbia University Contributions to Education*, No. 384. New York: Columbia University Press, 1929.

MANDLER, G., "The Interruption of Behavior," in D. Levine, ed., *Nebraska Symposium on Motivation*. Lincoln, Nebraska: University of Nebraska Press, 1964.

MARTINEAU, P., *Motivation in Advertising*. New York: McGraw-Hill Book Co., 1957.

MCGINNIES, E., "Emotionality and Perceptual Defense," *Psychological Review*, 56 (1949), 244–51.

MORGAN, J. J. B., *Keeping a Sound Mind*. New York: Macmillan, 1934.

NAFE, J. P., "An Experimental Study of the Affective Qualities," *American Journal of Psychology*, 35 (1924), 507–44.

NOWLIS, V., "The Development and Modification of Motivational Systems in Personality," in M. R. Jones, ed., *Current Theory and Research in Motivation*. Lincoln, Nebraska: University of Nebraska Press, 1953.

NOWLIS, V., and H. H. NOWLIS, "The Description and Analysis of Mood," *Annals of the New York Academy of Science*, 65 (1956), 345–55.

OLDS, J., and P. MILNER, "Positive Reinforcement Produced by Electrical Stimulation of Septal Area and Other Regions of Rat Brain," *Journal of Comparative and Physiological Psychology*, 47 (1954), 419–27.

OSGOOD, C. E., "The Nature and Measurement of Meaning," *Psychological Bulletin*, 49 (1952), 197–237.

OSGOOD, C. E., and G. J. SUCI, "Factor Analysis of Meaning," *Journal of Experimental Psychology*, 50 (1955), 325–38.

PRIBRAM, K. H., "The New Neurology and the Biology of Emotion," *American Psychologist*, 22 (1967), 830–38. (a)

———, "Emotion: Steps Toward a Neuropsychological Theory," in D. C. Glass, ed., *Neurophysiology and Emotion*. New York: The Rockefeller University Press, 1967. (b)

PULLIAS, E. V., "Masturbation as a Mental Hygiene Problem: A Study of the Beliefs of Seventy-Five Young Men," *Journal of Abnormal and Social Psychology*, 32 (1937), 216–22.

RAPAPORT, D., *Emotion and Memory*. New York: International Universities Press, 1950. (Menninger Clinic Monograph Series, No. 2, 1942. Unaltered edition, 1950.)

RICHTER, C. P., "Increased Salt Appetite in Adrenalectomized Rats," *American Journal of Physiology*, 115 (1936), 155–61.

———, "Total Self-Regulatory Functions in Animals and Human Beings," *The Harvey Lecture Series*, 38 (1942), 63–103.

ROTTER, J. B., "Level of Aspiration as a Method of Studying

Personality: I., A critical review of methodology," *Psychological Review*, 49 (1942), 463-74.

ROUTTENBERG, A., "The Two-Arousal Hypothesis: Reticular Formation and Limbic System," *Psychological Review*, 75 (1968), 51-80.

SCHACHTER, S., and J. E. SINGER, "Cognitive, Social, and Physiological Determinants of Emotional State," *Psychological Review*, 69 (1962), 379-99.

SCHUMANN, F., "Beiträge zur Analyse der Gesichtswahrnehmungen," *Zeitschrift für Psychologie*, 23 (1900), 1-32.

SELYE, H., *The Stress of Life*. New York: McGraw-Hill Book Co., 1956.

SHERIF, M., and H. CANTRIL, *The Psychology of Ego-Involvements, Social Attitudes and Identifications*. New York: John Wiley & Sons, 1947.

SHERRINGTON, C. S., *The Integrative Action of the Nervous System*. New Haven: Yale University Press, 1911.

SPITZ, R. A., "The Smiling Response: A Contribution to the Ontogenesis of Social Relations," *Genetic Psychology Monographs*, 34 (1946), 57-125.

STRONGMAN, K. T., *The Psychology of Emotion*. New York: John Wiley & Sons, 1973.

SYMONDS, P. W., *The Dynamics of Human Adjustment*. New York: Appleton-Century, 1946.

THOMAS, W. F., and P. T. YOUNG, "Liking and Disliking Persons," *Journal of Social Psychology*, 9 (1938), 169-88.

TINBERGEN, N., "Social Releasers and the Experimental Method Required for Their Study," *Wilson Bulletin*, 60 (1948), 6-51.

TITCHENER, E. B., *Lectures on the Elementary Psychology of Feeling and Attention*. New York: Macmillan, 1908.

TOLMAN, E. C., "A Behavioristic Account of the Emotions," *Psychological Review*, 30 (1923), 217-27.

TOMKINS, S. S., *Affect, Imagery, Consciousness: Vol. I, The Positive Affects, Vol. II, The Negative Affects*. New York: Springer, 1962 and 1963.

TROLAND, L. T., *The Fundamentals of Human Motivation*. Princeton, New Jersey: Van Nostrand, 1928.

ULRICH, R. E., R. R. HUTCHINSON, and N. H. AZRIN, "Pain-Elicited Aggression," *Psychological Record*, 15 (1965), 111-26.

WATSON, J. B., "A Schematic Outline of the Emotions," *Psychological Review*, 26 (1919), 165-96.

WEIL, J. L., *A Neurophysiological Model of Emotional and Intentional Behavior*. Springfield, Illinois: Charles C Thomas, 1974.

WENGER, M. A., "Emotion as Visceral Action: An Extension of Lange's Theory," in M. L. Reymert, ed., *The Mooseheart Symposium on Feelings and Emotions*. New York: McGraw-Hill, 1950.

WESSMAN, A. E., and D. F. RICKS, *Mood and Personality*. New York: Holt, Rinehart and Winston, 1966.

WILSON, W., "Correlates of Avowed Happiness," *Psychological Bulletin*, 67 (1967), 294–306.

YOUNG, P. T., "An Experimental Study of Mixed Feelings," *American Journal of Psychology*, 29 (1918), 237–71.

———, "Studies in Affective Psychology: IX, The Point of View of Affective Psychology," *American Journal of Psychology*, 42 (1930), 27–35.

———, "Relative Food Preferences of the White Rat," *Journal of Comparative Psychology*, 14 (1932), 297–319.

———, "Relative Food Preferences of the White Rat, II," *Journal of Comparative Psychology*, 15 (1933), 149–65.

———, "Laughing and Weeping, Cheerfulness and Depression: A Study of Moods among College Students," *Journal of Social Psychology*, 8 (1937), 311–34.

———, "Emotion as Disorganized Response: A Reply to Professor Leeper," *Psychological Review*, 56 (1949), 184–91.

———, *Motivation and Emotion: A Survey of the Determinants of Human and Animal Activity*. New York: John Wiley & Sons, 1961.

———, "Hedonic Organization and Regulation of Behavior," *Psychological Review*, 73 (1966), 59–86.

———, "Affective Arousal: Some Implications," *American Psychologist*, 22 (1967), 32–40. (a)

———, "Palatability: The Hedonic Response to Foodstuffs," in C. F. Code et al., eds., *Handbook of Physiology*. Baltimore: Williams and Wilkins, 1967. Section 6, Vol. 1, *Alimentary Canal*. (b)

———, "Evaluation and Preference in Behavioral Development," *Psychological Review*, 75 (1968), 222–41.

———, "Feeling and Emotion," in B. B. Wolman, ed., *Handbook of General Psychology*. Englewood Cliffs, N.J.: Prentice-Hall, 1973. (a)

———, *Emotion in Man and Animal: Its Nature and Dynamic Basis*, 2nd rev. ed. Huntington, New York: Robert E. Krieger Publishing Co., 1973. (b)

YOUNG, P. T., and J. P. CHAPLIN, "Studies of Food Preference, Appetite and Dietary Habit: III, Palatability and Appetite in Relation to Bodily Need," *Comparative Psychology Monographs*, 18 (1945), 1–45.

YOUNG, P. T., and C. H. MADSEN, JR., "Individual Isohedons in Sucrose-Sodium Chloride and Sucrose-Saccharin Gustatory Areas," *Journal of Comparative and Physiological Psychology*, 56 (1963), 903–909.

READING SUGGESTIONS FOR ADVANCED STUDY

For further discussion of topics treated in this book see: P. T. Young, *Emotion in Man and Animal: Its Nature and Dynamic Basis*, 2nd rev. ed. (1973). Also my earlier text may be useful: P. T. Young, *Motivation and Emotion: A Survey of the Determinants of Human and Animal Activity* (1961). A point of view similar to my own has been clearly expressed in an essay by the late J. Konorski entitled, "Study of Behavior: Science or Pseudoscience," in J. W. Cullen, ed. *Legacies in the Study of Behavior* (1974).

For students of physiological psychology who are concerned with problems of motivation and emotion and who have a background in neural anatomy, I recommend: J. L. Weil, *A Neurophysiological Model of Emotional and Intentional Behavior* (1974). This book describes current research and is especially noteworthy for the treatment of nonspecific neural systems that activate positive and negative processes of pleasure and unpleasure. A collection of experimental and critical papers relating to emotion can be found in: D. C. Glass, ed., *Neurophysiology and Emotions: Proceedings of a Conference under the Auspices of Russell Sage Foundation and the Rockefeller University* (1967).

The following works are useful for orientation and theory relating to emotion: M. B. Arnold, *Emotion and Personality: Vol. I, Psychological Aspects, Vol. II, Neurological and Physiological Aspects* (1960). S. S. Tomkins, *Affect, Imagery, Consciousness: Vol. I, The Positive Affects, Vol. II, The Negative Aspects* (1962 & 1963). J. Hillman, *Emotion: A Comprehensive Phenomenology of Theories and Their Meanings for Therapy* (1961). K. T. Strongman, *The Psychology of Emotion* (1973).

These works have extensive bibliographies which point to specific sources.

Index of Authors

Index of Subjects*

* The content of this index is limited to the text exclusive of appendixes.